"This book packs a perfect combination of cutting-edge theories; engaging stories; and real-time, practical tools. Guaranteed to leave readers with an increased capacity to communicate, respond, and love better!"

—**George Faller, LMFT**, EFT trainer, president of the New York Center for Emotionally Focused Therapy (NYCEFT), and coauthor of *Emotionally Focused Family Therapy*

"Having worked with Jennine on dozens of articles for some of the biggest magazines in the US and UK over the past fifteen years, I have seen firsthand how her unparalleled knowledge, empathy, and compassion can heal hearts, mend bonds, and rebuild relationships. *Help for High-Conflict Couples* is a clear result of decades of research and hard work, and it will surely change lives."

—**Brenda Della Casa**, author, journalist, and self-esteem and empowerment coach

"This book is a great resource for high-conflict couples. Written by two very competent, experienced emotionally focused therapy (EFT) therapists, the book lays out in simple but powerful terms how to use EFT principles to end high conflict and replace it with a loving, secure bond. This book will be a valuable resource for years to come."

—**Scott R. Woolley, PhD**, distinguished professor at Alliant International University, EFT trainer, and founding director of the San Diego Center for EFT and TRIEFT Alliant

T0038415

"A treasure trove of tools to increase emotional safety, de-escalate conflict, and stop damaging relationship cycles, *Help for High-Conflict Couples* sheds light on how couples can shift to a secure attachment by getting to the core emotional roots of their issues. Compassionate and relatable in tone and style, the authors gently encourage readers to dig deeper into their relationships and into themselves, through the lens of EFT."

—**Lisa Brookes Kift, MFT,**
    founder of www.loveandlifetoolbox.com

"Estes Powell and Wielick's expertise and conversational tone create an approachable path to healing through EFT. Their compassion and experience shine through the text as a safe guide toward results."

—**Jordan Brown,** book reviewer at @getlitbookclub

"This isn't just another relationship book. It's a practical guide with helpful tools and exercises to turn conflict into connection and get your communication back on track."

—**Michael Fulwiler,** founder of Fulwiler Media, author
    of *Therapy Marketer*, and former chief marketing officer
    of The Gottman Institute

Help for
High-Conflict
Couples

Using Emotionally Focused Therapy
& the Science of Attachment to
Build <u>Lasting Connection</u>

JENNINE ESTES POWELL, LMFT
JACQUELINE WIELICK, LMFT

New Harbinger Publications, Inc.

Publisher's Note

NEW HARBINGER PUBLICATIONS is a registered trademark of New Harbinger Publications, Inc.

New Harbinger Publications is an employee-owned company.

Copyright © 2024 by Jennine Estes Powell and Jacqueline Wielick
New Harbinger Publications, Inc.
5720 Shattuck Avenue
Oakland, CA 94609
www.newharbinger.com

All Rights Reserved

Cover design by Amy Shoup

Acquired by Jess O'Brien

Edited by Cindy B. Nixon

Library of Congress Cataloging-in-Publication Data on file

Printed in the United States of America

26   25   24

10   9   8   7   6   5   4   3   2   1   First Printing

For our clients, who inspire us every day.

Contents

Foreword   vii

Introduction   1

Chapter 1   What's Love Got to Do with It?   12

Chapter 2   Why Emotionally Focused Therapy?   39

Chapter 3   Cooling Down   55

Chapter 4   Caught in the Cycle: Identifying the Pattern   82

Chapter 5   Trauma's Impact on Connection   97

Chapter 6   Resolving Past Hurts   123

Chapter 7   Let's Talk About Sex   146

Chapter 8   Celebrate, Connect, Advance   167

Afterword   179

References   181

Foreword

When I first developed emotionally focused therapy (EFT) in the 1980s, I had no idea how or if it would be embraced by my fellow clinicians aiming to improve the lives of couples in distress through the means of strengthening their connection, and I had no expectations for how EFT might be applied beyond my own office.

EFT has shown its effectiveness for high-conflict couples; once we have a map and see through the conflict to the pain of disconnection, then renewed loving connection is possible. This book provides practical tools and exercises for couples to explore their contribution to conflicts and move toward a more secure and lasting connection. It also integrates attachment theory, and together with EFT, both are highly effective approaches to couples therapy.

The authors are powerfully compassionate and insightful, with a deep understanding of the challenges couples face in high-conflict relationships. The book's use of real-life examples and storylines is also a significant strength, as it helps readers feel seen and understood in their struggles. Additionally, the book's emphasis on the journey couples takes as they work to restore their relationship is likely to provide hope and predictability for those who are considering therapy.

I'd recommend this book to both couples struggling in their relationships and to the various helping professionals dedicated to therapeutically navigating couples through their struggles. Both will find much to learn in these pages, many helpful practices to start applying, and more than enough hope to reignite belief in the potential and the power of any high-conflict couple to resolve their conflict.

—Dr. Susan M. Johnson, EdD
Developer of Emotionally Focused Therapy

Introduction

Hey, reader! We see you. Not to make assumptions about you, but you are probably exhausted and burnt out in your relationship, tired of trying, at your wit's end with your partner, and maybe even contemplating ending the relationship. Getting chewed out, blamed, or left right in the middle of a conversation is getting to be too much. Or maybe the remote control has been thrown way too many times and the yelling and cursing are getting way too old. We get it.

As two licensed marriage and family therapists, we know the suffering that couples are in by the time they come to us—knee-deep in conflict and as their last resort—because we see it every day. When things are bad, they're really bad. And the hard part is that when things are good, they're really good. Your list of complaints is valid and needs fixing quickly. Every move counts when couples are in high distress. As therapists, we work on getting to the root of the issues and fixing why things got disconnected in the first place, and that is exactly what we are going to do in this book.

We see your pain, we see your struggle, and that is why we created this survival guide: to provide you with some concrete steps so things can get better. So thank you for your trust and congratulations on taking charge of your life and working to make something different for yourself and for your relationship. This takes courage, bravery, and strength.

One of the most painful things for high-conflict couples is losing hope. Maybe you can relate. Many couples have tried everything—handling conflict differently, attempting to repair things over and over, reading multiple books, seeking advice from friends and family or even multiple therapists—and nothing has worked. This hopelessness can be heartbreaking and cause feelings of despair. The research on attachment tells us that relationships are the most important part of our lives as human beings, for our wellness as well as for our survival. When you feel the pain of your relationship with your partner slipping through your fingers every day, it's only natural and normal to feel devastated about the prospect of losing them—no matter how bad things have gotten.

But know this: Hurt people heal every day. Hurt relationships heal every day. It happens all the time. We see it before our very eyes, so we know it's possible. In the wise words of an esteemed colleague, "Although you don't know if it's going to work for you, you have to work as if it's going to" (Woolley 2022). This is the attitude toward therapy we're going to advise you to have throughout this book. Take the information, suggestions, and exercises being shared with you here into your life as if this interventional approach is going to work. Just put all decision making about your relationship on pause for now. Regardless of what you ultimately decide about the relationship, to stay or to go, act as if, right now in this very moment, finding help and healing is possible—because it is.

What Is a "High-Conflict Couple"?

High-conflict couples are similar to "normal" couples, just with the metaphorical volume turned up. This heightened level of conflict might look like out-of-control outbursts, frequent slides into disconnection or silence, disappearing acts, or quick flare-ups with a lot of yelling. According to Lisa Palmer Olsen and Scott Woolley, two experts on emotionally focused therapy with high-conflict couples, the fighting in these relationships, in comparison with lower-conflict couples, tends to (1) escalate quicker, (2) escalate more often, and (3) escalate with higher intensity (Palmer Olsen 2022; Woolley 2022).

People in high-conflict relationships also tend to be inflexible in their dynamics; by this we mean their patterns of reacting and emotional vibing with each other are apt to be pretty rigid. In other words, during heated times, their reactions are typically strong and consistent, and they are unable to easily change their responses even when they see how they are impacting their partner.

Some people don't consider how they are impacting their partner and are unable to hear their partner's experience, no matter what their partner does. If they do understand that they are negatively impacting their partner, they don't really care at that moment because their hurt is just so big— they are unable to see past their own pain and understand their partner's pain. It becomes difficult to change their reactions during the hard times in the relationship. It's almost as if no matter what they do or what the other person does, the interaction isn't going to change. They are fixed in their rigid behaviors. Not only are they unable to "reach" for their partner in a way that is tender, but they are also unable to change how they are *responding* during the fight. This is important, because psychological flexibility—the ability to change one's response, reaction, perception, or understanding of their partner and therefore change their relationship dynamic—is the key to healthy relationships.

As just mentioned, we can think of our behaviors toward our partners as figuratively "reaching" for them—we are trying to reach them, hoping that this reach has some kind of impact, will make some kind of meaningful connection or difference in the interaction. In high-conflict couples, no matter what they do, this reach doesn't tend to impact the dynamic enough to make a difference.

Maybe you have experienced this. Maybe you've first tried to reason with your partner, then to talk and explain things to them, but when that didn't work, you moved on to screaming, crying, threatening to leave, pushing, shoving, slamming doors, throwing a plate at the wall, or the silent treatment. And yet none of this seems to get through to your partner or make any difference in the pattern between the two of you. *This* dynamic is the very definition of a rigid state.

In these relationships, a key component of relational well-being, vulnerability, is seen as being very unsafe, an opening for an assault or an attack, and not worth the risk. And this feeling is valid—high-conflict couples have experienced so much emotional assault that it *isn't* yet safe for either partner to consider opening themselves up fully to the other.

The lack of hope we mentioned earlier is also common in these couples. This is partly because of the inflexible pattern between them that has not changed after many years of trying to do something different. Hope also dissipates because many forms of treatment for couples have no clue as to how to get to the root of these issues and actually help.

This is where we come in.

Some therapists miss the bigger picture of what is going on in relationships by slapping a diagnosis on one or both of the clients' foreheads. A diagnosis might make sense of a client's symptoms and reactions, but it misses the *process*—what makes a person tick, why their body responds in a certain way to triggers, what they need for long-term change. A diagnostic label leaves the client walking out of the office not feeling understood and seen. They're just a disorder or disability now, and the therapeutic focus shifts to fixing their problematic behaviors and thoughts rather than the larger relational dynamic in which they exist.

You or your partner may have received a diagnosis from a professional, or you may have diagnosed each other with something like narcissism or borderline personality disorder—trust us, we hear these diagnoses thrown around our office every week! An accurate diagnosis might provide some comfort or logic to symptoms (not just for the clients, but for therapists as well), but it misses the mark in terms of the relationship dynamic between two people.

We see conflict in a different way—not as a manifestation of psychological diagnoses. Don't get us wrong: identifying a mental health issue can be extremely important and it can be extremely helpful in treatment, but in the context of a relationship, we see a larger picture. Conflict and high escalation happen for a reason, not just because your partner is "crazy." By taking this viewpoint, we can see more of the true person outside their behaviors and conflict. We can look at what's happening for each person that contributes to the larger pattern between them. Focusing on diagnoses looks to the individual first rather than to the couple in relationship.

So in this book, we take a bigger-picture perspective: we examine the process, not just the two people engaged in that process. You and your partner are more than just a diagnosis or bundle of psychological terms. We want to help you see yourself and your partner as human beings with hearts in pain that have learned specific ways to cope in the world.

How We Plan to Help You

In this book, we dive into the larger *why* of your relationship: understanding who you and your partner are and what influences the intense reactions you both have. We then present a step-by-step plan to get you out of high-conflict mode by using the concepts and stages of the research-based experiential theoretical model known as emotionally focused therapy (EFT). We will be looking at your relationship through the lenses of attachment science, neuroscience, and the science of emotions alongside EFT in order to provide you and your partner with some structured support to escape your unhappy patterns and rigid relationship dynamic. For years, both authors have tried working with different theoretical models to help our couples, but we were unable to meet goals and find relief for our clients *until we discovered EFT*. Once we adopted this approach, we hit client goals and saw long-term change in action. This was our inspiration for the book.

First, we will calm down your heated fights quickly. The first few chapters provide you with some tools to improve relationship communication, soothe your nervous system, and regulate your body, along with some effective strategies to cool things down between the two of you. We then explore the deep root issues at play by examining your life experiences and attachments, past and present, and how they impact both your and your partner's abilities to connect; the aim is to establish more secure communication between the two of you so you can rebuild trust and resolve past and present problems.

Throughout the book, we want to help you create a totally new relationship dynamic with your partner. We don't mean just tweaking a few things or changing a few behaviors here or there. We're talking a complete overhaul—working to construct a totally new cycle between the two of you that goes far deeper than just your behaviors.

You may be wondering how we plan to accomplish such a large task, given the current conflict you're locked in. Well, think of this process as building a house: instead of renovating a creaky, haunted house that is falling apart, we want to start from scratch and help you to erect a whole new dream home. We'll map out the floor plan, complete with dimensions, installation methods, and techniques. We'll help you gather the materials, lay the foundation, frame the walls, make sure the structure is sound, and, at the end, we'll even help you decorate it so it looks good for the long run!

But in this analogy, note that you're the subcontractor—you're the one who will be doing the work within your relationship and with your partner every step of the way. We can provide only the building plans and instructions, with lots of guidance and emotional support along the way (we've got a lot of that to give!), but you're the one who will be wielding the tools in hand.

As we proceed through the book, we'll be sharing lots of case histories from our therapy work with clients. It should go without saying that we have changed all the names and some specifics to protect the sacred confidentiality of our clients, but the topics, themes, dynamics, and experiences illustrated in these personal stories are directly applicable to high-conflict couples. It's important to include real-life anecdotes in a book like this so that you can integrate the material into your own relationship to the greatest degree possible.

You'll also encounter lots of exercises and activities along the way, all intended to guide you toward experiencing your relationship differently. We'll be asking you to practice making changes within yourself (and, ideally, within your relationship) to ensure the changes stick long-term.

Research on neuroplasticity shows that human behavior can change only through new experiences (Lamagna 2022), which is a two-step process here: first, you'll *learn* the new information through the text sections, then you'll *experience* the new information in the exercises as you practice applying it. Doing so engages both the right and the left sides of the brain and thus promotes the growth of new neural connections, which in turn create change in your dynamic within your relationship.

Given this, it's preferable that you and your partner both do the exercises, so we recommend that your partner also reads the book before you practice the exercises together. When you have both been exposed to the tools and skills herein, you'll know how to cool off and show up for each other so that the exercises will be more effective. They're centered on finding new ways of having conversations that will draw the two of you closer together, so joint participation is optimal.

And yet we understand that you may very well be reading this book on your own, that there's just *no way* you're going to get your partner to read it. That's perfectly okay! We know from applying EFT for many years that it takes only one person to step outside of the dynamic with their partner to make a change in the relationship. So if you're approaching this book on your own, know that the awareness and growth you'll gain will mostly be yours, it's true, but it can still be an incredibly effective and worthwhile experience in creating change in your relationship.

Either way—whether you journey through this book as a solo traveler who then takes what you've learned to your relationship or whether you take the journey together—*don't skip the exercises!* They're an integral part of providing you with a new experience of yourself and of your partner en route to creating long-term changes in your relationship.

To complete the exercises, you'll need a journal. Because there's no designated workbook, you can just create one for yourself using a blank book, a notebook, a pad of paper, a computer file, or even the notes app on your phone. Just keep it handy as you navigate the chapters and expect to add to it as you go.

How Did You Get Here?

There are three main reasons why a couple becomes a "high-conflict couple": (1) unprocessed past trauma; (2) betrayals in the relationship (which we'll refer to throughout this book, in therapist lingo, as "attachment injuries"); and/or (3) the "negative cycle," or negative behavioral pattern of interacting, that the couple has fall into. In the negative cycle, the way each partner relays information creates conflict, which then leaves each partner not getting their needs met.

High conflict in couples can be caused by one of these things on their own or by a combination of any of these things. We'll cover all of them in this book, using EFT to offer concrete and research-based approaches to solve conflict in three ways:

1. Helping *you* gain a better understanding of what is happening inside yourself emotionally, physically, and psychologically

2. Helping *you* gain a better understanding of what your partner is experiencing emotionally, physically, and psychologically

3. Learning how to respond to your own emotions and to your partner's reactions in a way that will decrease the fighting and increase the closeness and comfort

Notice the emphasis on "you" in this list: Wouldn't it be great to be able to point your finger at your partner and say all of your problems are their fault? Have them take the responsibility for all of the discord between you? Like most people, you've probably attempted that from time to time, and sometimes it even seems true—like the issue at hand *is* entirely their fault. We're in relationships too, and we understand the temptation to see ourselves as perfect and our partner as the flawed one. But we also know that's definitely not the reality. Working through conflict requires us to step out of a "my pain trumps all" perspective into a space that can flexibly accommodate *both* realities: our own reality and pain *and* our partner's own reality and pain—in other words, getting out of that rigid stance.

One common theme we notice in high-conflict couples is that each partner doesn't seem to know how much they impact the other partner. Before we go even one word farther in this book, then, we want to stress this: *you have more impact on your partner than you realize.* Just having that awareness—that you *do* have an impact on your partner, both positive and negative—is the beginning of the change you want to see. When you increase your awareness in this way, you then begin to notice how *you* are feeling and reacting toward your partner, how *your* responses may be impacting them and contributing to the pattern of conflict between you. There's never just one party involved in an ongoing relationship cycle.

Is This Book for You?

There are three A's that can prevent couples counseling from being effective: active abuse, active affairs, and active addictions. When we say "active," we mean that they are still happening today—the affair is still going on, the addiction is still out of control, or the abuse is still happening. In these cases, a higher level of treatment or support than what's offered in this book is called for.

But if you've experienced addiction, abuse, or affairs that are in the past or have recently ceased, then this book readily applies. These relationship injuries can greatly influence the high conflict between the two of you and are, in fact, pretty common influencers in high volatility. So rest assured that you are not alone in suffering from these injuries and that we have a road map you can follow to help. Any one of these issues needs to be addressed in a way that resolves and corrects the issue, leaving you both feeling successful.

If the issue is still active in your lives, however, it's a whole different ball game. Let's talk a little about why the approach mapped out in this book is not intended for active abuse, affairs, or addiction.

Abuse comes in multiple forms. Someone can be abused physically, sexually, emotionally, or financially. Of couples entering therapy, 50 to 65 percent of them report some form of interpersonal violence, including pushing, restraining, and hitting (Slootmaeckers and Migerode 2019). At times, these episodes arise from mutually escalating interactions, each partner influencing the other, caused by negative communication patterns. If your simple need for safety is being threatened, it is not possible to address the emotional needs in your relationship with this book. Instead, seek out counseling. If applicable, reach out to a domestic violence hotline (the National Domestic Violence Hotline at 800-799-7233 is a 24/7 resource) to access the resources and support you need, create a safety plan, and get as many people on your team as possible. Only after the abuse stops can you move forward with a tool like this book to help repair your relationship.

An active affair is what we call a "competing attachment," as it's competing with you for your partner's attention and affection. The one being cheated on will never feel safe as long as there's another person who has a strong or stronger pull on the relationship. During an active affair, the ongoing deception, lies, and betrayals can never lead to decreased conflict—they only fuel the volatility. So if there's still a third party in the picture, that needs to be addressed first before this book can be of use. If an affair happened in the past, however, either recently or long ago, this book can be extremely helpful for you and your partner to move past it toward healing and growth.

Lastly, addiction. No matter how talented a couples therapist is, addiction will win every time—it's another kind of attachment that competes with you for your partner's attention and affection. In people with addictions, the impulsive and compulsive thoughts, emotions, and behaviors to seek out the object of addiction (whether it's alcohol, drugs, porn, or sex) cause betrayal and block the ability to be fully present and available to their partner—they simply cannot properly emotionally regulate and tune in to their partner. If you or your partner has an active addiction that has you caught in a "this will be the last time" cycle (though it never is), treatment for the addiction is a mandatory prerequisite before even considering applying the concepts we set forth here. If either of you is currently in therapy for the addiction and the addiction is currently under control, though, then this book can be a wonderful resource for both of you in healing from the injuries addiction causes.

Tying It All Together

At the end of each chapter, you will see us tying together the concepts discussed to consolidate big ideas into bite-sized pieces. For now, here's how you can help us help you: give yourself three months to move through this material and actively work toward creating a different dynamic with your partner. During this span, your job is to just focus on your side of the street. If the volatility in your relationship doesn't change after three months, you may need to assess whether staying in the relationship is the right decision for you.

But we're not there yet, right? We're just getting started. So for the time being, just know how happy we are that you are here with us, dedicated to working on improving your relationship with your partner. Let's begin.

CHAPTER 1

What's Love Got to Do with It?

Another door slams, more f-bombs are dropped, and the fighting is just going in circles again. The attempts to be seen and understood by your partner are exhausting and get you nowhere. Each fight impacts how much, if at all, you open or close your heart to connecting to your partner in your relationship. The louder you scream to be heard, the farther away they move. The more your partner shuts down, gives you the silent treatment, or attacks you, the more it reinforces your beliefs about them: *I can't count on them. They are not safe for me. I won't let them hurt me anymore.* This is an excruciatingly painful place for couples to be. Some people don't fully understand why they or their partner goes from zero to sixty so easily, why certain topics just lead to disconnection, or how they can make their communication better. On the other hand, some people know *exactly* what the problem is ... it's their partner! (Can you relate?)

The depths of the pain you're experiencing may be from what you or your partner did (or didn't do), from feeling alone in the relationship, or from being super frustrated that no matter how loud you yell, they never listen. Whatever the cause is, your overwhelming emotions are valid and real. You may be completely done with all the fighting and toxicity. Picking up this book may have taken the last bit of energy you have to work on the relationship. You likely didn't pick it up without trying a ton of different tactics to fix things first. You have probably worked extremely hard trying to change the fighting and to communicate differently. Your attempts matter; they show you're still fighting for the relationship. If you are feeling exhausted and can see no path to improvement, keep reading.

This chapter will provide you with "building plans" for your new dream home—the materials that will form the foundation for creating a new dynamic with your partner. You can think of this chapter as the "why" for the rest of the book, because if you don't understand why you are doing what you are doing, then building a brand-new structure with your romantic partner becomes even more challenging. You will learn background information and research on love, conflict, attachment, and emotions—all part of the building plans that will pave the way toward success in the rest of the book.

Escalated couples typically consist of very passionate people with big, loving hearts, but for one or both partners, the ability to stay regulated emotionally and consider the other person's feelings is lacking. It's like the volume is turned up on their emotional reactions, while vulnerability and empathy are turned down. Everything during a fight becomes extreme, it's hard to press the reboot button, and each partner finds it difficult to respond with tenderness and calmness. Vulnerability can be unsafe, as it can lead to an opening to be wounded badly.

This fast-igniting fire within a high-conflict couple can stem from many issues, such as years of unmet needs and untended longings. It can be from hard experiences in the past, maybe with family or in past relationships. Another cause for the fire can be going through difficult times in the relationship in the past, like affairs, betrayals, experiences with substance use, or any form of abuse (called "attachment injuries"). Certain behaviors can feed the fire, such as partners who go "radio silent" or pull disappearing acts. A partner can be so fearful of abandonment that they give ultimatums, threaten to leave, or, worse yet, threaten to take their own life. Any or all of these issues cause a lot of turbulence in the relationship, and if left unresolved, they can lead to even more issues in the future.

It can be very hard to tease out what's really going on in the present moment from the past junk that's getting in the way. Throughout this book, we'll go into more specifics about the flames that feed the fire of volatile arguments and teach you how to address them.

As you go through these chapters, the content may bring up difficult feelings and truths about your relationship. It may shine a light on things you don't want to see or admit. Please, *do not fall into a shame spiral* over this! You deserve to have this information. It is important to understand what is going on in your life in order to find your way through it. You should be proud for fighting through these difficult truths for your relationship. If things get to be too much, feel free to set the book down, take a pause, then pick it back up when you're ready to continue. And remember, you can't force your partner to change, but you *can* work on your side of the street.

Let's start with an exercise to help you acknowledge the current status of your relationship and assess its volatility.

EXERCISE: Temperature Check

Below is a list of situations that can cause distress in a relationship. We're not trying to stir up the pot, but it's important to bring the issues you're facing to the forefront so you can enhance your understanding of what's going on. Acknowledging what's happening in your relationship and taking accountability for your part in problematic issues are essential elements of the healing process. Just like in a maze, you first need to know where you are in order to get out. So grab your journal and jot down which of these statements you relate to, or make a photocopy of this page and circle the statements that resonate:

- My friends and family have no idea how bad my relationship actually is.

- My partner doesn't listen to me, ever.

- Storming out of the room or leaving is a common move my partner or I make when things get tough.

- At some point in our relationship, trust has been broken.

- One of us heats up so fast, gets extremely angry, and explodes over the little (and big) things.

- Keeping our emotions in check is very hard.

- We have a sexless marriage.

- We have turned into roommates (and I hate it).

- Our communication during hard talks sucks.

- My partner flies off the handle when angry (yells, breaks things, punches walls, and so forth).

- My partner and I curse and call each other names.

- I am scared often.

- We blame each other.

- I feel defensive most of the time. I am always ready for an attack.

- Small issues cause big fights.

- Our fights start on a topic, and then past issues come up.

- The breakup/divorce card gets thrown out when we fight.

- We question our ability to get through difficult times.

- We question our relationship when the going gets tough.

- We haven't touched for a long time.

- My partner won't talk to me.

- My partner or I tend to avoid conflict at all costs, agreeing to things we don't really agree on.

- My partner says one thing and then does another.

- I am on edge, waiting for the next shoe to drop.

Now rate your overall relationship on a scale from 0 to 10 (with 0 = not distressing at all and 10 = very distressing). How much do these points of conflict impact you? How upsetting or frustrating are these issues for you?

The number you assigned to your distress level is the current "temperature" of your relationship.

Next, think about what your relationship *does* bring to your life—the positives. What keeps you there, willing to keep fighting for its survival? Write down at least three reasons for still fighting for this relationship (and they have to be more than your kids or your pets). When things get tough in the upcoming chapters, refer back to this list as an anchor to remind you why you're still committed.

Boundaries and Stability

For those in agony, drowning in doubt, and continually facing intolerable conflict, boundaries are going to be critical for establishing a sense of stability. Trust can't be built on faith that things will change; like all change, it has to be *experienced*. Taking the leap to address your relationship issues will require a level of boundary setting, which sets up a safety net for both of you. You set boundaries with your partner, and then your partner creates emotionally safe experiences for you, and vice versa. This means putting down the booze, quitting the threats to leave, and stopping interruptions when the other is speaking.

We'll start with two boundaries for each of you:

First boundary: If your fights are intense, DO NOT fight in front of the kids. They should not be exposed to your conflicts. No exceptions.

Second boundary: Refrain from escapist and elevating substances—alcohol and drugs—while you are working on the relationship. You both need clear heads to respond to each other properly. (Don't worry, you're not saying goodbye to martinis forever. Just for now.)

TOOLS FOR YOUR TOOLBOX:
Setting Boundaries in Three Steps

Here's how to set a boundary in three simple steps. We call this the "safety sandwich" because the expressed boundary is couched between two statements that not only provide context for the boundary but also more importantly, cushion the boundary between two validating statements that soften the tone and set the boundary up to be heard by the listener more successfully:

1. Opening safety statement: a sentence that validates your partner as it relates to the boundary

2. Boundary statement: the "meat" of the sandwich that expresses your desired boundary in clear, direct, noncritical, and nonblaming language

3. Alternative solution statement: a concluding thought that offers an alternative to more successfully resolve the current conflict by prioritizing the relationship and inviting more closeness with your partner

Note that these statements do not have to rigidly adhere to just three sentences—it's the content and the order that matters more than how many periods are in your boundary dialogues.

Examples of Safety Sandwiches:

- "I know you are upset. I want to hear what you're saying right now, but yelling curses at me is not okay; I can't hear you through your anger. We will revisit this once things cool off."

- "I understand that you want to resolve this issue now. But we need to press pause until we are both sober. It's important to me that we're both clearheaded when we talk about this so we can resolve this as a team."

- "It's okay that you feel upset right now as we're discussing this, and I need you to stop threatening to leave to help me feel safe. This is a hard topic for us, and how you feel matters to me. Let's just take a little break to calm down."

- "I can see that you are hurt and angry, and I want to hear about what you're feeling. But it really scared me when you punched a hole through the wall, and I'm concerned about our safety. That is not okay. It needs to stop. We need to press pause right now so we can cool off. I want to hear what you have to say when we are calmer." (Note: This situation is getting too close to violence and must stop immediately before any more progress is attempted.)

- "I understand that you want us to resolve this issue now. I am getting frustrated, and I need to take a break to cool off. I want to speak to you about this calmly in one hour so things can be productive and successful for us."

- "I understand that you need to cool off right now, and it's okay for you to take a break. I need reassurance that you will come back to continue talking. Let's decide on a time to revisit this discussion together."

TOOLS FOR YOUR TOOLBOX:
Taking a Negotiated Break

Notice how many of the examples above entailed taking a break from the heat of the argument. So it's already time for another tool you can use as you work to dismantle the pattern of conflict that's been established in your relationship.

When should the two of you take a break, and what should that break look like? Well, whenever you notice your partner's reaction becoming escalated as a conflict continues to rise, that's a good time for either one of you to set a "pressing the pause button" boundary and take an agreed-upon break for a minimum of thirty minutes, as it takes the body approximately twenty-three minutes to regulate and return to baseline after experiencing a threat. (For someone with a history of trauma, this may take even longer.) Pro tip: This is the perfect amount of time to watch a half-hour episode of the show you're currently bingeing on Netflix, so take this span to calm down, regulate your body, and not ruminate about the conflict.

When you call a break, start by indicating to your partner that you *need* a break so that you can really hear what they're saying and show up as your best self to solve the conflict together. This kind of language is critical to helping your partner still feel connected to you while you're taking a break. So *never* ghost them—don't just leave the room without explanation or with a hostile exit. And before you temporarily take some space—this is the most important part—make sure you set an exact time to reconvene. Remind your partner that you are *protecting* the relationship by stepping away and *you will come back.*

Here are the rules during your break:

1. You and your partner do not engage.

2. You do not ruminate on the conflict.

3. You cope with your own emotions.

What do we mean by "you cope"? We offer several tools and scenarios in chapter 3 that specify steps you can take and measures you can practice, but in general, dealing with your own emotions means taking charge of your side of the street. You cannot control your partner, but you *can* control your responses and reactions to them in any given situation. How you alone act and react has the ability to change the dynamic with your partner, so try out some of the recommendations in chapter 3 to see what works best for you. The goal of taking a break is to get yourself to a place where you are feeling emotionally centered and calm again before making any decisions on what to do next or how to move forward with the conflict with your partner.

THERAPY HELPS If it is feeling emotionally unsafe to open up in your relationship, seek out therapy while navigating the content of this book. Bringing the exercises into your counseling can maximize your progress and provide some support along the way. Oftentimes, couples in highly conflictual relationships become isolated, and their problems become highly secretive. Research shows that having a grounding and healthy third party involved can significantly de-escalate these interactions (Palmer-Olsen 2022).

Understanding Love

To understand conflict, we must first understand love. Sigmund Freud put it perfectly: "We are never so vulnerable as when we are in love" (Johnson 2013, 17). Humans are pack animals—relationship with others is in our DNA, and it opens us up in a way that ignites vulnerability and deep feelings. We don't just want love, we *need* it. Research on love and relationships affirms that humans need others for survival (Bowlby 1982; Johnson 2008; Bretherton 1992), and it's terrifying to live without such loving connections.

Clinical psychologist Sue Johnson is the creator of EFT, and she says that romantic partners are like "two porcupines huddled together on a winter's night" (Johnson 2013, 17). Being close is necessary for survival so you don't freeze, yet in getting close to others, we run the risk of getting poked and experiencing hurt. So love and security are survival needs like food and water, yes—our species wouldn't have lasted very long without them, after all—and yet so many of us surround ourselves in "quills" for protection. This push and pull between the need for love and closeness and the terror of being hurt (or getting hurt again) lies at the root of all high-conflict couples.

Understanding Attachment

To understand love, we must first understand attachment. Attachments are the emotional bonds you have with other people, and research shows that our attachment patterns are learned in childhood (Cassidy, Jones, and Shaver 2013; Rees 2007). Like love, these attachments, or bonds, are imperative for human beings. In historical terms, they increased the chances of survival—to be nurtured and protected by those around you, your clan. And in the context of this book's theme of the emotional bond between two romantic partners, attachment styles are critical because they play a large role in how each individual communicates and handles conflict. If you had poor examples or experiences of connection in your childhood, problems bonding and being close to others in your family home, this will show up in your adult relationships. But don't let this freak you out. *Attachment styles can be unlearned and relearned.* One goal of this book, in fact, is for you to experience a new attachment style with your partner.

Attachment theory, developed by British psychologist John Bowlby, helps us make sense of our need for love and security beyond inborn instincts, because it identifies typical styles, or patterns, for connecting with others, such as anxious attachment style, avoidant attachment style, or secure attachment style (Bowlby 1982). Some people follow more than one pattern, as when both anxious and avoidant attachment combine to create the disorganized attachment style. All the different labels aren't as important right now as knowing that the secure attachment style is what we're after: that's the one that creates feelings of security with our partners.

Why is secure attachment important? Research shows that folks with secure attachments are more likely—first as children, then as adults—to explore, learn, and relate; they have an increased sense of well-being, motivation, feelings of safety and trust with others, stress regulation, adaptability, and resilience (Cassidy, Jones, and Shaver 2013; Rees 2007). Basically, secure attachment produces a laundry list of good things we all want. So that's what we'll be working on with you: getting you and your partner to progress to a secure attachment style using some research-based steps.

Understanding Insecure Attachment Styles

Insecure attachment styles typically come in three varieties: anxious, avoidant, and disorganized. Those with an anxious attachment style tend to feel on edge and to question both themselves and their partners. Anxiety is the body's way to keep itself safe, always scanning the immediate environment for threats and being on high alert to every possible danger. These folks usually criticize, follow their partners from room to room during arguments, and don't want to take breaks from hard conversations.

Those with an avoidant attachment style, on the other hand, tend to turn away from their partners to cope with difficult emotions. These folks often shut down, look away, disengage, or leave during conflict. They also work hard at maintaining peace, avoiding arguments, and disregarding their own feelings and needs. They're the "Everything's fine!" people.

Those with the disorganized attachment style are challenged on both ends: they experience anxiety in their relationships *and* they seek to avoid the anxiety whenever and however they can. Their fear of abandonment is high, influencing extreme reactions. They want closeness terribly, yet they are also terrified of it. They are the "Come close; no, go away!" people. It can feel disorienting to be on the other side of this, with partners feeling like they're getting mixed messages as to what their mate wants from them.

Quick Reference: Attachment Patterns

Here's a summary overview of the attachment styles we'll be repeatedly referring to throughout the book.

Anxious Attachment:

- *What it looks like:* doubting, asking questions over and over, following, internet stalking, or repeatedly checking a partner's social media; bringing up the same issues over and over again, questioning both partners' reactions; fear of abandonment; inability to take a break or stop a conflict interaction; discomfort or fear around being alone or being apart

- *What it sounds like:* criticizing or blaming language, such as "You always do that" or "You never listen to me;" poking and questioning, such as "Why did you just look at your phone?" or "Why are you ignoring me?"

Avoidant Attachment:

- *What it looks like:* conflict avoidance, fear of conflict, people pleasing to avoid confrontation, withdrawing, stonewalling, the silent treatment; discomfort with or fear of vulnerability and getting "too close" to others; "just going with the flow," not sharing feelings or needs

- *What it sounds like:* defensiveness, minimizing, trying to shut down the conversation; pacifying with such statements as "It's fine" or "It's not a big deal;" often saying "I don't know" or saying nothing at all

Disorganized Attachment:

- *What it looks like:* intense mood swings, being the hero and then quickly changing to the villain (with no in-between), self-harm, constantly seeking attention, extreme reactions, self-destructive behaviors, explosive anger, difficulty trusting others

- *What it sounds like:* contradictory comments of wanting closeness but then pushing it away; "I hate you, don't leave me" reactions and statements; bringing up health concerns or threatening to take their own life (in hopes for closeness); saying things like "I don't know who I can trust" and "I'm afraid of being abandoned"

Secure Attachment:

- *What it looks like:* confidence, calmness, and comfortability, even in times of conflict; ability to be close to and engage with others, as well as be separated from others; sense of safety in oneself and in relationships; reciprocal interactions with partner; ability to share feelings and ask for needs in a relationship; ability to trust

- *What it sounds like:* "I see you are upset;" "I feel like we can talk this out reasonably;" "Thank you for sharing that with me;" "I am here for you;" "I need this today;" "I feel hurt, can we talk about this?" "I trust that you are doing your best"

Attachment Needs

In addition to having a typical style for connecting with others, we all have *attachment needs* that underlie our behaviors. These include such elemental desires as the need for love, closeness, and comfort, and they influence our actions toward others, particularly our partners. These needs hold true throughout the life span; it's a common misconception to think that as we get older, our emotional needs for closeness and comfort diminish. On the contrary, research shows that we have the attachment needs of acceptance, love, comfort, and closeness at any age—it's how our brains are wired.

Babies deprived of close contact in the first six months of their lives grow up to be psychologically damaged. This yearning to feel loved by others, and to love others, is one of the greatest and most natural primal human needs there is, and it's a predictor of human happiness (Raghunathan 2014). Because love is such a basic human need, it's only natural that when this attachment need is not met or is threatened, severe pain and distress occur. This is when people act out in conflictual ways and where the high-conflict couples disconnect.

Your Response Counts: Attachment in Action

Our emotional experience of our partner, our perception of how important we are in the relationship, and the security of the relationship all play a critical role in a couple's attachment to one another. The more connected and secure you feel, the less reactive you will be. The more you experience disconnection, the more distressed you will be. EFT helps couples feel more securely attached and less disconnected from each other.

A famous developmental psychology experiment from the 1970s conducted in the lab of Dr. Edward Tronick illustrates the paramount importance of attachment (Goldman 2010). In what's known as the "Still Face Experiment," lots of babies and their caregivers were gathered together. First, the caregivers were instructed to interact with their babies face-to-face while behavioral responses and reactions were observed. When a baby would make a sound, their caregiver would smile with delight and enthusiastically say something encouraging, like "Yay!" In return, the baby would smile, the pair would coo at each other, the infant would try to touch their caregiver's face, the caregiver would take the baby's hand, and so forth. In other words, the interaction was reciprocal—going back and forth equally—even before a tiny baby has had time to learn about social interactions. This ability to be social and to connect reciprocally to others is hardwired into the biology of the human brain, part of our innate makeup.

In the next phase of the experiment, the caregivers were told to stop responding to their babies. They were to hold their faces completely blank for a few minutes, regardless of what the babies did. At first, the babies tried anything they could to elicit a response from their caregivers, to reinstate the reciprocal interactions—they made adorable cooing sounds, they waved their little hands, they cried, and then they positively screamed. But after several minutes of no response, the babies turned their heads, positioned themselves away from the caregivers, and appeared withdrawn, depressed, and hopeless. These findings have been replicated again and again, demonstrating the deep pain humans have lodged inside them when we do not get the emotional responses we seek from our attachment figures.

The Still Face Experiment evidences just how much responses count in human interactions. Receiving a response from others that shows us we matter, are seen, loved, and important, is a biological attachment need we all share, whether we're seven months old or seventy years old. Couples use various ways to attempt to reach their partner, to obtain a response from them. When we get no response, our emotions flare up and we quickly react: we increase our volume, change our facial expressions, raise our tone, make threats, become short, and eventually withdraw by turning away to disconnect from the pain. So if you shut down to avoid conflict, that can actually cause more escalation in your partner. All of these knee-jerk reactions are an attempt to gain connection—just like babies learn at an incredibly early point in their development, *any* response is better than no response. So remember: *your response counts.*

EXERCISE: Your Attachment Style

We've assembled a list of statements intended to increase your awareness of your own attachment style—to explore your areas of strength as well as areas that could benefit from growth. When you see the word "others," this refers to your close friends and family, in addition to the statements that focus on your relationship with your partner.

In your journal, respond to each statement by indicating how much you agree or disagree with it on a scale from 1 to 10 (where 1 = strongly disagree and 10 = strongly agree). Before you dive in, take a deep breath. Be kind to and compassionate with yourself whatever your responses. Knowledge is power, and this information will help you decrease the conflict in your relationship in the long run. Note that if you're currently upset with your partner, you'll rate the relationship differently than if you're not, so it's best to undertake this exercise when you're feeling neutral.

Your Typical Attachment Areas of Strength and Growth:

1. I share my fears and vulnerable emotions with others.

2. I give verbal and physical affection to others without anxiety or fear.

3. I can clearly share when I need to feel closeness with others. I am not snappy, distant, or impatient when I really wish to feel close.

4. I feel secure and am never on the lookout for the "next shoe to drop."

5. I prioritize my self-care and my needs before those of others.

6. I give others compliments throughout the day (and mean them).

7. I say I'm sorry when I make a mistake or do something wrong. I don't dwell on it after.

8. I am able to stay calm when others share their hurt with me.

9. I am able to stay emotionally present during hard talks with others. I don't quickly explain, defend my position, or leave.

10. I grew up with a family that showed me how to have healthy disagreements and stay connected.

11. I grew up without any traumas (such as abuse, attacks, car accidents, life-threatening experiences, or emotional or mental neglect, such that love was withheld or manipulations were common).

12. I am able to set healthy boundaries and say no when needed to my coworkers, friends, and partner.

13. When I share my vulnerable emotions, it draws others close to me.

14. I am not irritable or fearful when others want to be close to me. I stay calm.

15. When I get reassurance from others, it comforts me and calms me down quickly.

16. I usually don't second-guess myself.

17. I don't have anxiety that causes me to disassociate, space out, or have panic attacks.

Scoring Information:

Add up your scores and use the scale below to assess your areas of strength and opportunities for growth:

- Score 17–65: Your attachment style is on the insecure end. Your ability to feel fully secure in yourself and with others is difficult. Learning healthy attachment with others will be your area of growth (and this book will help you with that!).

- Score 65–100: In some relationships, you are able to feel secure, and in some, you are not. Consistency in your attachment to others (who are safe) will be your area of growth.

- Score 100+: Your attachment style is closer to a secure attachment. Your focus will be on bringing this strength to the forefront of your relationship with your partner, not just reserved for friends and family.

Next, reflect on your score in your journal. Which questions did you score the highest on and why? What are your attachment strengths? Celebrate yourself here! In what ways can you see your overall attachment style showing up in your relationship? Our own attachment styles work hard to protect us in different ways and have good intentions, but they can also make relationships feel very difficult. Understanding your own style is so important because it plays into your negative pattern with your partner. The more insight you have about your attachment to others, the more it can help you take steps to improve your side of the street.

Daniel and James's Story

The relationship between Daniel and James serves as a fitting example of how core attachment needs and styles can lead to escalating conflict in a couple. This young couple who met in college has been together for seven years and they cohabitate. Daniel grew up in a religious family in the Midwest, where he felt unaccepted and criticized for his sexuality. On some subconscious level, he learned he had to perform, perfect himself, and pursue others in order to receive love and acceptance.

James, meanwhile, grew up in Los Angeles within a family that accepted his sexuality. His large, Italian family showed him lots of love—and also lots of conflict! Screaming matches between his parents were a nightly occurrence. On more than one occasion, things got physical between his parents, which is when he would hide in his room. On some subconscious level, James learned that conflict was something dangerous to be avoided at all costs.

This pair gets along great … most of the time. They have mutual respect and love, they enjoy the same activities, and they love to laugh together—until their different attachment needs are threatened. When that happens, things escalate fast, which is common in volatile couples, *where the conflict doesn't creep in, it races in like a sports car already doing sixty miles per hour.*

For example, Daniel likes a clean house; James doesn't seem to mind either way. Daniel has asked James on far more than one occasion to help with the dishes and keep the kitchen tidy, and James has agreed to do so. But one morning, Daniel comes into the kitchen to find the sink overflowing. Again. He immediately starts throwing out passive-aggressive comments at James, accusing him of not only not caring about the dishes, but also not seeming to care about anything. Defensively, James yells back that it's only a pile of dishes, that Daniel needs to calm down, and that this is not a big deal at all. Then he walks away.

Daniel follows him, continuing to yell, asking James why they're even together because James obviously doesn't care about him or their home—if he did, they wouldn't have to have this same conversation a hundred times. James doesn't even turn around; he just gets in his car and drives off.

What's Really Going on Here?

So you don't need a psychology degree to realize this isn't just about the dishes, right? Daniel and James are actually playing out a typical theme we see in highly escalated couples: on a deep level that each partner is not even aware of, they have different views of what arguing means to them in terms of safety and danger. Conflict arises because of these differently held meanings.

In this case, Daniel's attachment needs, because of his upbringing, are to feel seen, heard, and accepted for who he is. He wants to know that his requests are valid and important. This translates to a core need in his relationship of feeling securely connected to his partner, that he can count on him. But when James (unintentionally) sends him the message that his requests are not important—what's the big deal about some dishes in the sink?—this touches a deeply painful place in Daniel that sets off his insecure attachment style and threatens his attachment needs.

For his part, because of his own upbringing, James has an avoidant attachment style that aims to fulfill his needs for peace, connection, and freedom from conflict. When he shuts down in the face of one of Daniel's outbursts, it's because he senses danger, a threat to their attachment, so he attempts to cool things off by temporarily disengaging with him to protect their closeness. It's not that James withdraws because Daniel doesn't matter to him; it's that Daniel matters *so much* to him that he can't bear the disconnection, so he does what he knows how to do to stop it—first by trying to explain the situation away before it can blow up into a big fight, then by physically leaving the interaction once the fight is unavoidable.

James's response is what threatens Daniel's own attachment need for closeness and comfort even more, so the interaction escalates. This is the "negative cycle" they're caught in (something we'll discuss more in later chapters). It's important to note about such quickly escalating conflicts that the parties involved are not making intentional choices. Rather, they're just immediately reacting according to their attachment styles based on instinctual responses to threatened attachment needs.

Safety with Others: Green, Yellow, and Red People

Different people can elicit different reactions within us. With some, we feel confident getting close to them, completely comfortable spending time with them and sharing all parts of ourselves with them. With others, we feel iffy—although we enjoy their company, full disclosure isn't part of the equation with them; there's something lacking in terms of feeling emotional safety, and we pick and choose wisely what we do share. And still others make us want to pump the breaks, slow down quickly, or even disconnect altogether. In this way, connecting with others is like approaching

Help for High-Conflict Couples

a streetlight, where the colors signal to us how we should proceed with "green people," "yellow people," or "red people."

A "green" person is someone with whom you feel safe moving forward, just like you know you can keep your foot on the gas pedal at a green light (you might even speed up). You want to explore the world with them, continue to spend time with them, and share new adventures and experiences with them because it feels safe to do so. *They* feel safe. You allow yourself to open up and be vulnerable. They are predictable, they show up for you, and they're always there for you. They have your back, and in moments of pain, they help ease it for you and work to make things right with you. You feel soothed by and comfortable with green-light people, and the feeling is mutual—the love, respect, and disclosure here are reciprocated. When you're with the green people in your life, your body isn't tight or on edge; you can take your armor off and breathe easily.

A yellow light signals to proceed with caution. With "yellow" people, you'll want to assess what's going on and determine whether you should speed up or slow down. We can love yellow people dearly and they can love us dearly in return, but that doesn't mean they *always* show up for us— more like they only show up for us when we *really* need them. They sometimes get caught up in their own stuff and leave us hanging, yet they can really be there when it is critical.

Sometimes these relationships stay more on the surface—you don't really talk about deep stuff and sometimes you even feel judged or criticized by them. These people actually come from a good place, but you can only rely on them in certain ways. Like, they might not keep secrets totally safe, so we may not feel inclined to be completely vulnerable with them and we don't fully share ourselves with them. When we're with a yellow person, the walls in our body feel halfway up—we're slightly tense at times, but we still feel in control of our own safety. The bottom line with yellow people is that you can still keep them in your life—they're great to invite to a barbecue—but you'll want to selectively filter parts of yourself in their presence and not fully trust your heart in their hands.

Then, of course, there's the red light—where you just stop. You do not and should not move forward. No new adventures with "red" people, no new scenery to take in with them. That's because red people have proven to be unsafe to you; they've hurt you in ways that damage you deeply and thus they are dangerous to you. These are the people who don't show up for you, are unpredictable, and are only looking out for themselves. The damage they cause can be physical, mental, emotional, sexual, or financial. In the presence of a red-light person, your stomach turns, your alarms go off, and your gut tells you something is wrong. These people should not be in your life, period. If there's no escaping them, you need to be prepared whenever you encounter them by emotionally zipping yourself up, protecting yourself, and surviving the exposure until you can get back to safety and take care of yourself.

We discussed this streetlight analogy with Daniel and James during a counseling session with them and led them through the exercise below that we're going to have you complete in a moment. What Daniel discovered is that some members of his family are red people to him, because of their continued lack of acceptance of him, and some members are yellow—those with whom acceptance still feels conditional. James concluded that all his family members are yellow for him: he knows they love one another, but he cannot trust their consistency and predictability.

Both Daniel and James were grateful to discover that their community of friends is filled with attachments they've formed with "green people." And, interestingly, both men learned that they're yellow for each other: they deeply love each other, but they're not yet at the point where their walls are all the way down; it doesn't yet feel entirely safe to be completely vulnerable. Our goal is to get them—and to get you and your partner—to be "green people" for each other.

EXERCISE: Colorize the People in Your Life

In your journal, list all the important people in your life, including your partner, and assign a color that best fits your experience of them.

How many "green people" surround you? If there are none, that's okay, that's honest. Now is the time to start seeking and nurturing green relationships.

How about your "yellow people"? No need to toss them out of your life just because you've acknowledged that they're a gossip or that your friendship is built on little but history. Instead, enjoy what you can with these people, while also realizing that they are not completely safe for you.

Do you have some "reds" in your life? If so, consider prioritizing your safety first and eliminating these relationships to the greatest extent you can. If you cannot eliminate them, be mindful of protecting yourself when you must be exposed to them.

Know that it's common to want to categorize people in the green group, only to become extremely disappointed later when they fail to show up for you. This is normal—you're not alone in this. So this exercise isn't about idealizing (or demonizing) the relationships in your life; it's about acknowledging the capacities other people have in their attachments to us so that we can better manage our expectations of them.

Lastly, what color is your partner? What color are you for them? Can you be safe, consistent, and predictable for them, provide them with the closeness and comfort they crave? What improvements can each of you make to become "green" to each other?

Why We React the Way We Do

Humans naturally have very adaptive, self-protective mechanisms to help them survive. The most well-known survival responses are called "fight," "flight," "freeze," and "appease" (referenced moving forward as "fight-or-flight" responses for ease). This is relevant here because these reactions play into the patterns of communication and attachment we have with our partners when conflict swoops in. These survival responses are ingrained and come from the oldest and most primal part of our brains—many times, awareness of these responses is outside of our consciousness and choice. So when people hurt us (either intentionally or unintentionally), or when we *perceive* that someone has hurt us (this is an important distinction), we automatically, and naturally, react to the behavior.

The more we perceive someone as dangerous, the more ammunition we need to protect ourselves. The brain turns on its alarm, we mentally categorize this person as "unsafe," and we arm ourselves against them by reacting with a fight-or-flight response as an automatic defense mechanism—as a barrier around our hearts. Think of it this way: your body is doing its job by trying to keep you safe, even if the symptoms of that protection are emotionally uncomfortable. Unfortunately for relationships, the symptoms of these responses are typically further escalation of conflict and consequent disconnection. Understanding these responses is an important prerequisite to following our blueprint for how to decrease the conflict in your relationship.

Fight

The "fight" survival response might sound negative, but it can actually be essential for getting through difficult times. When you are physically, verbally, or emotionally attacked, this response aims to defend you against a very real threat. We're no longer cavepeople fighting off ferocious beasts in the wilderness, but if Grandma constantly belittled you as a child, after a while, the automatic response to become reactive to her may have welled up inside you; instead of cowering under her criticism, you started talking back and saying hurtful things to her in return as an attempt to protect yourself. Or a teenage boy who's been repeatedly hit by a parent—eventually, he will tire of the abuse or be unable to tolerate it any longer, and his anger will cause him to fight back. It's only natural to want to protect ourselves and fight off threats, so in instances like these, the fight response is a very adaptive way for a child to cope with their situation so they don't drown and possibly even perish in an environment they cannot escape.

While recognizing that the fight instinct can be adaptive, however, it is not always helpful, useful, or productive in our later relationships, especially with our partners. Here, the response can manifest as pursuing, following, explaining, blaming, yelling, throwing, hitting, or kicking. It is usually not the intention of the partner to bring forward this response, but it understandably comes across as dangerous and painful to the other partner and can create a further disconnection in the relationship.

Flight

The next adaptive survival response, flight, compels us to protect ourselves by *escaping* a situation that feels overwhelming, scary, and hurtful. This doesn't just equate to physical escape—we can flee mentally and emotionally, too, through such means as using substances, spacing out, shutting down, going quiet, dissociating, scrolling on social media, or distracting ourselves by always "staying busy" and being "on the go." Have you ever seen a spooked cat run away to seek out shelter? It finds a dark place in a corner for comfort. Its body is on high alert, with a fast heart rate, rapid breathing, and a poofy tail.

Like a scared cat, people use the instinctive coping skill of flight (either literally running away or figuratively in their minds) to get out of a potentially dangerous situation, calm their body down, and get back to safety again. Like a husband, overwhelmed by his wife's constant criticism and attacks, who stays silent and daydreams about his favorite hobby during their big arguments or a wife who heads to the mall for some retail therapy when her husband once again comes home from work in a rage. In these examples, running away is an adaptive response to remove oneself from conflict and distress, find shelter, and create safety. Unfortunately, the flight response in a relationship can send the message that you've abandoned the relationship and leave your partner feeling all alone. The result? Escalated arguing and further disconnection.

Freeze

Freezing is another adaptive survival skill. Your body becomes paralyzed, devoid of any response, and your mind draws a blank. The idea is, the less movement, the quicker the threat will pass. When a deer sees headlights, it freezes to keep it from being spotted. When a camper encounters a bear in the woods, they often freeze, hoping the bear will just keep moving. Freezing serves the function of not engaging with the perpetrator; by avoiding additional conflict or distress, the individual is hoping the attack will quickly dissipate (Raypole 2021). It also serves the function of giving the individual's brain and body more time to prepare and plan for next steps.

Picture a child with terrible stage fright going blank during the performance of a school play—a response to the threat of being stared down by so many people. We see this in relationships, too: in response to conflict, some people shut down, not necessarily to avoid it, but because their mind is frozen and they feel paralyzed, unable to come up with a response. It's an adaptive survival instinct, the brain's way of trying to help the body not be noticed. In relationships, though, freezing can send the signal that the person is not in the conversation at all, just doesn't care, and this leaves their partner feeling all alone, which—you guessed it—escalates the conflict.

Appease

Appeasing is the fourth and least-talked-about survival response, another attempt to find an alternate path to safety. When a person appeases, they fawn all over the person threatening them as a way to keep that person happy and calm. This can end up looking like people-pleasing tendencies, codependency, pacification, not sharing feelings and needs, and avoiding conflict by sugarcoating situations. It is adaptive because it keeps the threat at bay by disarming it—it's a means to keep the other person happy so that conflict can be avoided altogether (Raypole 2021).

Consider a boyfriend who's constantly being chastised by his girlfriend; in response, he agrees with her and laughs along, even though he doesn't believe what she's accusing him of or find it funny in the least. He praises her wit to avoid further criticism. He refrains from sharing his own thoughts and feelings to not set off her anger. In a romantic relationship, appeasing can be devastating because there is a lack of authenticity and real communication. So there's no true intimacy or trust. The appeaser is never truly known by their partner, resentment builds, and so does the distance between the couple, filled by emptiness.

What's Attachment Got to Do with This?

So how do these instinctual human reactions play into the attachment dynamics of romantic relationships? Well, any of them can be perceived as a threat to the attachment needs we talked about earlier. The more experience someone has with rather unsafe "yellow people" and definitely unsafe "red people," the more skilled they become at protecting themself. When this is the framework in which they operate, it can become automatic for them to just expect hurt to come their way. And so they react as though danger is always right around the corner.

If you or your partner endured difficult relationships early in your life, you may find yourselves "stuck" in one of these survival response modes in the face of conflict or challenges, utilizing the same tactic over and over again that helped keep you safe (either emotionally, spiritually, mentally, or physically) in your past. This contributes to creating a repetitive cycle—looping interactions—with your partner. And it's not just our attachment needs that merge with our automatic responses; our attachment styles do as well. For instance, avoidant people will tend to lean on freeze or appease survival techniques, while anxious people often rely on appeasement and fight responses when feeling threatened.

Let's revisit Daniel and James to explore this further. During their conflicts, Daniel's go-to response is to fight. We can see this as he yells, follows James from room to room, and tries to get him to engage. Daniel is not actually trying to fight James: he is trying to fight for a *response from* James—a response that will meet his attachment needs of being seen, heard, and secure in the relationship. He has an anxious attachment pattern, learned in childhood, that causes him to perpetually seek safety.

James's automatic survival response is flight. He gets defensive, dismisses the problem, shuts down, and then literally flees. James is not trying to leave Daniel, but he is trying to escape the *conflict* with Daniel, trying to meet his own attachment needs of closeness and harmony with his partner. He has an avoidant attachment pattern, learned in childhood, also in an effort to maintain safety.

Can you see how each of their survival reactions plays off the other? It's like a ping-pong match between these two reactions, each unsuccessfully trying to meet the underlying attachment needs of closeness and comfort with each other.

Tying It All Together

In this chapter, we introduced how our past and present experiences with different attachment styles and needs, different kinds of people, and different adaptive survival strategies all intermingle to create the ways in which we show up in our most significant relationship with our partners. Knowledge is power, and the more you know and understand about yourself and your relationship, the easier it will be to build this new dream home we are working toward constructing for you.

So far, we've just gone over the outline, the rough building plans, to develop a fundamental understanding of what is currently going on, so we can then help you dismantle it all and build something new in its place. In the upcoming chapters, we'll talk about the tools and building blocks that will make this possible.

CHAPTER 2

Why Emotionally Focused Therapy?

"So, what brings you into therapy during this time?" asks Rochelle, the EFT therapist who looks at the new couple sitting across from her on the couch with curiosity and openness. The man, Sean, with his arms and legs crossed, looks uncomfortably to the corner of the room, admiring the clock. His partner, Tamara, sits on the edge of her seat. "He is so mean to me. I think he has an anger management problem! I gave him this ultimatum to come here and have you fix him or else I said I would leave." Sean has been silent up until this moment; now he speaks firmly, "You think *I* have an anger management problem? Really? *Me?!* Have you looked in a mirror?" He rolls his eyes. Tamara looks at Rochelle, basically asking her to throw her a life raft. "Do you see what I have to deal with? He's so distracted with work, he doesn't care about me, and he's impossible to talk to about anything. I really think he's just selfish, and that's the problem." What does Rochelle, as an EFT therapist, do next?

This chapter brings us to why you are here. Your partner isn't just anyone to you—there is a special connection you have to each other, which makes the fighting between you even more frustrating. Somehow, someway, you got yourselves stuck in a negative communication pattern that just isn't working, like Tamara and Sean's. The more we react (or don't react) to our partners, the more it influences the other person's reactions.

Think of one of those baby mobiles that hangs over a crib: If you pull on one piece of the mobile, the entire thing reacts accordingly and continues to influence the movement of the entire fixture. If you think and respond differently toward your partner, it will force your partner to think and respond in a different manner too. Your connection with your partner is a bond that has meaning, and therefore, the behaviors and moves each of you make are very impactful on the other person. You both impact each other because there is a significant attachment between you that influences each other. So maybe this is an opportunity to start to consider how you have *more influence* on your partner and in your relationship than you originally thought!

> Rochelle leans into Sean, her curiosity and openness unhindered by the outburst. She says simply, "It seems like you're here because this has been really hard for both of you. Sean, how do you feel about being here today?" Sean looks surprised that she cares enough to ask how he really feels and hasn't written him off as a hopeless cause already. With an edge to his voice, he answers, "I'm pissed and I don't want to be here. She made me come here because she's always pissed off at me. I don't know what she wants. I'm so sick of it." He shakes his head and looks away again. Rochelle asks, "What's that like for you, to feel like she's always pissed at you?" His voice softens just a bit, and he says, "It's like I can't get anything right with her. There's no point in even trying."

Sean is impacted *because* Tamara matters to him. She is special to him. Yet at the same time, he is frustrated and feels like what he does isn't really making a difference. Tamara is fighting hard to make a connection by explaining (blaming); however, this strategy doesn't draw him closer to her.

So first things first: let's start putting all the attachment theory pieces of the last chapter together by incorporating them into the framework of a research-based solution that has helped unlimited numbers of couples: emotionally focused therapy. It is important to understand both attachment theory and EFT before we can use these concepts to make any changes in your relationship.

A Road Map of EFT for High-Conflict Couples

EFT is a research-tested and proven therapeutic theory that, when applied to couples therapy, can actually create positive and lasting change within a relationship (Wiebe and Johnson 2016). The short-term therapy approach was developed in the 1980s by Sue Johnson. EFT therapy techniques help couples understand what lies at the root of their emotional experiences, learn how to initiate communication in a more effective, vulnerable way, and ask for what they need clearly. It draws couples closer and responds to each partner's needs in ways that help create and strengthen a safer, fulfilling, and more positive bond.

In other words, EFT helps create a *secure attachment* in a relationship (Johnson 2008)—that's where we want to go, that's the "dream home" we talked about earlier—and it does so by following a very specific framework that consists of nine steps in three stages (Johnson 2013):

Stage 1: Stabilization

Step 1: Assess the couple's issues and each partner's individual issues (covered in chapters 1 and 2 of this book)

Step 2: Identify the negative cycle and attachment issues (chapter 4)

Step 3: Uncover underlying attachment emotions (chapter 3)

Step 4: Reframe the problem as the negative cycle (not the partners themselves) for the couple (chapter 4)

Stage 2: Restructuring the Bond

Step 5: Pinpoint deep attachment needs, fears, and models of self, then begin sharing new interactions from this place (chapters 5, 6, and 7)

Step 6: Promote acceptance of each partner's new experience and respond in a positive new way to these deep places (chapters 5, 6, and 7)

Step 7: Express attachment needs on an even deeper level (chapters 5, 6, and 7)

Stage 3: Integration/Consolidation

Step 8: Develop new positions in the cycle and enact new stories (chapter 8)

Step 9: Integrate new solutions (chapter 8)

(An expanded, annotated version of this EFT road map is available at this book's web page at: http://www.newharbinger.com/51932.)

Research has shown just how powerful relationships are in an individual's life, not only to mental health, but also to physical health, including depression, immune system functioning, and even heart disease (Gottman and Gottman 2000–2012). That's why it's so very important to strive for a secure attachment between partners—to fortify the structures of our unions when they are in disrepair, even completing rebuilding when and where necessary. It's worth fighting for the kind of connection we all want, the kind in which you feel like your partner has your back no matter what.

Starting to Heal the Fractures

Have you ever broken a bone? Without a cast on a broken arm, it is extremely painful, it impacts how you move the rest of your body, and it influences how you react to certain situations. To protect your injury, you may walk cautiously, keep your distance from other people, always be at the ready to jump if your arm is at all at risk of getting touched. Once a cast is put on it, your arm is much more protected and is able to start to heal. Your pain begins to decrease. The safer you feel with your arm inside the cast, the more it heals and the less protective you become.

EFT is like the cast: it identifies the relationship wound (the emotional disconnection) and provides a solution by creating emotional safety for the healing of the relationship. Once our couples are in sessions with us, they start to feel the safety of EFT around them, even if all of their issues aren't fully resolved yet.

> Tamara jumps in before Rochelle can respond to Sean. "He doesn't try; he literally doesn't do anything. He just comes home from work, plays video games, and ignores me. It's not because he's sick of trying. He's never even tried! He's just saying that because you're here." Rochelle ignores that last jab that Tamara threw in and dives into the core of the issue. "Tamara, what's it like for you when you feel ignored by your husband?" Tamara says definitively, "It makes me angry. It makes me feel so pissed off because all I do is cook and clean and do things for the kids, and I'm sick of it." Rochelle asks, "When you feel ignored, what message do you get?" Tamara softens a bit: "It feels like he doesn't even care about me."

Feeling cared for, during the good and the bad times, is one of those core, innate biological attachment needs we all have. Couples can lose the sense of being important to each other when they are in a fight. One benefit and often unexpected result of using EFT is that after completing treatment, couples frequently find themselves closer and happier in their relationship than they were before the conflicts even began. This is because EFT helps couples get to the underlying issues and resolve them; as the couple learns to create a safe attachment and repair emotional hurts in the relationship, a new cycle of positivity and connection can emerge.

Sean looks surprised and confused by Tamara's comment, like he can't imagine that it's even important to her at all to feel cared for by him. He jumps in, "It's not that I don't care. I'm just sick of getting yelled at all the time. I don't want to deal with it anymore. Anything I do makes it worse." Tamara looks directly at him for the first time since the session started, right in the eye, studies him suspiciously, seeming utterly surprised that he began to explain that the reason for the disconnection in their relationship is not because he does not care about her. Rochelle reflects back on what Sean is saying, with "So it sounds like for you, Sean, it's not that you don't care about Tamara; it's that you care a lot—so when you get the message that you aren't getting it right, it gets hard for you. You hide away, try not to make things worse and to avoid more conflict with her. Is that right?" Sean nods and his shoulders relax, looking relieved. "Yes, exactly. That's exactly what it's like." The wheels in Tamara's mind start turning.

People don't like fighting, but some people really despise conflict. Underneath Sean's anger and withdrawal is a side of him that his partner doesn't get to see. He is impacted by her emotionally in a very big way and therefore avoids conflict with her to prevent things from getting worse. It's like a fire. When a fire starts up, people react in different ways to this danger: some will try to put the fire out, whereas others will wait for the fire to burn out.

Tamara, for example, tries to put out the flames by talking about the fire, increasing her tone, blaming, and explaining more—all in an attempt to connect. But all this does is push her husband farther away. Sean does the opposite: the flames seem impossible to put out, so he waits for the fire to burn out on its own before he attempts to reconnect. He knows the fire can keep going and hours of conflict can ensue. He doesn't trust that he and his wife can have a conversation that will be helpful in putting it out.

EFT helps identify the *motives behind* certain behaviors such as these, so both partners understand that they are working toward the same goal: resolution, getting the fire to go out. Some ways of getting the fire to go out are more effective than others, and that is what EFT teaches: the most effective way of putting out the fire.

High-Conflict Histories

Ian Witter, one of our EFT colleagues, says there's no difference working with high-conflict couples and other couples in conflict—it's just that the highly escalated pairs are more verbally critical about their issues. He explains that this is because these couples are more likely to have had "little t trauma" at some point in the past, which basically means that the symptoms they experience due to their trauma might not be enough to meet the full criteria for a post-traumatic stress disorder (PTSD) diagnosis, yet they are still impactful enough to cause these folks to be extremely defensive and quick to go on the attack during conflict with their partners. "Fortunately, EFT was created to work with clients experiencing distress in their relationship, and can be very effective in working with highly escalated couples," he writes (Witter 2017, 1).

Our history plays a part in this. The more stable and secure the connections we had with our family growing up or in our past relationships, the more likely we are to regulate our bodies and handle difficult situations in our relationships. The more chaotic our past situations were (without being properly healed), the more our bodies learned how to protect themselves and quickly go into survival mode to get us through.

Integrating Attachment with EFT

This brings us back to talking about attachment. The old-school belief in psychology was that you needed to be fully secure in yourself before you could have a healthy relationship with others. The thought process went something like this: You can't be impacted by other people. Be your own person! Be independent! However, John Bowlby, the founder of attachment theory, found something different. His research discovered that early attachment experiences as a child will impact adulthood relationships. Early attachments will also impact how people emotionally regulate in relationships; "secure ones lead to emotional stability and insecure (anxious) ones to later difficulties" (Weizmann 2001).

Our attachment to others (starting from childhood) is vital for a sense of security within ourselves and how it plays out with others. Veronica Kallos-Lilly and Jennifer Fitzgerald have expressed it perfectly: "As humans, we need other humans, and not just any human, but humans who are special to us" (2015, 17). MRI scans have even shown EFT-associated changes in the way someone's brain responds to pain based on alterations in the attachment security of their significant relationship (Johnson and Greenman 2013).

So rather than needing to develop independently and be great on our own before we can connect properly with others, research shows that having safe, healthy, consistent people in our lives helps us develop a solid sense of self that provides us with a foundation for both successful independence and successful relationships. People with a secure attachment style are more comfortable in relationships, more comfortable on their own, and more able to explore the world around them.

A core tenet of EFT is that humans have an innate, biological need for secure attachments across their life span (Gehart 2014). Therefore, having an insecure attachment style can predict a decrease in relationship satisfaction (Johnson and Greenman 2013). Tamara and Sean are fighting for their connection in their relationship, but they're just not doing it in an effective way—and their attachment history is playing a part in this.

In their next sessions, Rochelle meets with Tamara and Sean individually to understand a bit more about who they are, what makes them tick, and why they are responding and reacting the way they do. She quickly learns that Sean's "normal childhood" was not so normal. "Everything was fine," he'd explain, but when they explored a little deeper, it turns out that what felt normal for Sean was explosive eruptions from his father. Sometimes these turned violent against his mom, his sister, and/or him if he wasn't careful. He instinctively, and luckily for his younger self, learned to stay out of the way, or it would just make things worse.

The more we make sense of Sean's way of protecting himself, by staying out of the way and disappearing, the more it connects the dots to what he's doing in his current relationship. He gets impacted by conflict with Tamara, and so he tries to get away from it. In his mind, conflict means danger. It doesn't mean he doesn't care about Tamara. He simply is fearful of the conflict and uses the tools he has acquired from his avoidant attachment style.

As for Tamara, her shock is visible when she not only hears Sean speak up about his experience, but when she also hears his words that start to *reframe* her experience—from an uncaring partner to someone who cares a lot about her. She softens to him. Now they are having a new interaction about their emotions that is deeper, provides a new perspective, and is more meaningful than just the content of their arguments. *This is what EFT is all about.*

Flying Trapeze Communication

If you've ever seen a flying trapeze act at a circus, you know there is a "flyer," a "catcher," and a net below them for safety. The flyer is the one who does the tricks, flying from one bar, letting go, and getting caught by the catcher on the other swinging bar. Several steps are required for the trick to work. First, the flyer stands on a platform far up in the air—twenty-five feet or more—toes hanging over the edge, holding on to a pole with one hand and the trapeze bar with the other, prepping for the feat. The catcher hangs upside down, swinging on a bar, pumping up the swing to be just the right height and pace, preparing to catch the flyer in midair. The flyer then informs the catcher they're ready for takeoff with "Listo!"

The catcher replies with "Hep!" as a way to say, *Jump, I'm ready for you!* The timing must be exact and perfectly in sync.

The flyer jumps, swinging through the air, and at the top of the swing lets go of the bar, flipping, and then reaches for the catcher, who is swinging toward them. The flyer's hands, arms, and body must be presented just right, making it safe for the catcher to grab their arms and swing through. If any of these moves are off, the trick can't be successful—and it can also be terrifying and dangerous for the acrobats. On the other hand, when done well, it is an incredibly graceful experience in which the acrobats create a connection together that is safe, fun, and beautiful.

It's the same for relationships. The way we inform, jump, reach, and catch our partner in times of vulnerability is vital. The way we jump to share our feelings, the way our partner is ready for us to take that risk, and the reaching in a way that allows one another to succeed—it all must align in perfect harmony in order for an interaction to be successful and safe. While navigating the different exercises and concepts in this book, we want you to think about the flying trapeze metaphor, how you can set both you and your partner up for success so that when you take that leap and jump toward each other, it can go well and bring you closer together in a shared experience of alignment and peace.

The first step to decreasing conflict is to avoid behaviors that make the relationship unsafe for vulnerability and connection. If the flyer's reach is unsafe, the catcher won't be able to catch them. In other words, avoid initiating communication with your partner by attacking, criticizing, or blaming them for how all of the relationship's woes are their fault (even if it feels like that). Similarly, if the catcher is unsafe in their catch, the flyer will fall.

So the first thing you want to do is to get control of *yourself*: Take a few moments at the edge of the precipice, breathe deeply, and be aware of how you are signaling to your partner that you're going to take a risk and jump. Stop pointing your finger at your partner. A trapeze flyer would never say, *Hey, catcher, you aren't doing it right!* The flyer has to focus on themselves, how to signal and jump when the time is right, and reach properly. It only takes one partner to step out of the fight. The trick is getting yourself to step out of your side of the pattern and calm yourself down so you're able to respond intentionally to your partner, even if you are upset. This then has the potential to change how your partner might respond to you. In the way that your response can change your partner's response, we can see how reacting thoughtfully and intentionally has the power to create a new, positive cycle between the two of you.

TOOLS FOR YOUR TOOLBOX:
Lay the Foundation

Houses are built on a solid foundation. In the metaphor we've been using for building a new dream house with your partner, think of the secure attachment you're working toward as the foundation. The more solidified the foundation, the stronger the house will hold up during storms. In her book *Hold Me Tight*, Sue Johnson (2008) explains that emotional responsiveness is the core foundation of a secure attachment and lasting love. She describes three main components of a secure and healthy relationship: accessibility, responsiveness, and engagement, otherwise known as A.R.E. Let's explore how these three elements can contribute to building a secure foundation in your relationship.

A = Accessibility: Accessibility is "staying open to your partner when you have doubts and feel insecure" (Johnson 2008, 49). It means fighting the urge to put up walls, shut down, or attack—and instead showing up. Be there when your partner is reaching for you. Be *available* and accessible, even in tough times.

R = Responsiveness: This means relying on your partner to *respond* to you emotionally. Read that again: to *respond*. This is knowing that your partner is responding to what you are sharing in an "I care about how you feel" kind of way. In Johnson's words, "It means accepting and placing a priority on emotional signals your partner conveys and *sending clear signals of comfort and caring* when your partner needs them" (2008, 50). Turn toward your partner and respond to them with tenderness, care, and interest. Show them you're there. This can be challenging during fired-up fights, but as in the Still Face Experiment we discussed earlier, the caretaker's responsiveness was critical to the baby's well-being—just as your partner's responsiveness is to yours.

E = Engagement: Being emotionally engaged is a "very special kind of attention that we give only to loved ones. We gaze at them longer, touch them more" (Johnson 2008, 50). Johnson calls this being "emotionally present." Recall how soothing and calming it was for the babies in the Still Face Experiment when they were receiving special attention from their loved ones. This is the same for you and your partner.

It's important to actively work on developing emotional security with your partner. It doesn't happen automatically, and love isn't enough to create the kind of emotional safety that a secure attachment can bring. If you turn to your partner for reassurance, comfort, and support and they are not accessible, responsive, and engaged, it makes sense that you would feel upset, hurt, afraid, or lonely. Feeling continuously ignored, dismissed, or uncared for will lead to insecurity in your attachment, and vice versa.

So from here on out, your responsibility in the relationship is to actively work on the three components of A.R.E. with each other. Show up. Make it safe and successful to be the flyer *and* the catcher.

EXERCISE: Who A.R.E. You?

A.R.E. is all about partners feeling like they have each other's backs, care about what the other is experiencing, and will show up for each other—during the calm, connected moments *and* during times of distress. Pull out your journal and take a good look at whether and how you are creating security for your partner. Ask yourself the following questions and write "yes" or "no" after each without looking ahead. Afterward, you can see how you rate in terms of your own accessibility, responsiveness, and engagement.

During Calm and Connecting Moments:

1. Do I show the emotional and physical affection I have for my partner?

2. Am I available to my partner when they are worried or concerned?

3. Am I easy to access? If I am not available, do I provide a time for when I can be available?

4. Do I show interest in how my partner is feeling?

5. Do I make my partner feel cared for, desired, and loved?

6. Do I actively respond to my partner's comments, interests, concerns, and questions?

During Difficult Times:

7. Am I able to regulate my emotions even if I disagree with my partner?

8. Do I show interest and care in what my partner is saying/feeling even if I don't agree with them?

9. If my partner is having a difficult emotion or a hard time, am I able to stay engaged with them and not shut down or leave?

10. Am I able to show affection (can be emotional or physical) to my partner during disagreements and fights?

Reviewing:

Accessibility: questions 2, 3, 7, and 9

Responsiveness: questions 4, 6, and 8

Engagement: questions 1, 5, and 10

How'd it go? What areas of A.R.E. are you strongest in? Weakest? What surprised you? Reflect on these findings in your journal.

Reactionary Patterns

When you are driving down the road and a big semitruck cuts you off, you're scared at first, but then you quickly shift to anger. You want to honk your horn, speed up, give the driver a dirty look, and mouth curse words through the window. Underneath your anger is a deep, vulnerable fear in response to the risk the other vehicle exposed you to. It was scary, right?

During fights with our partners, this exact same thing happens. We can be so fast to respond to our fears by yelling, being angry, or throwing out f-bombs, but all this does is keep our bodies in a fight-or-flight response—and make our partners stay on the defensive. Your reaction maintains a lack of safety in your relationship; even though you are *responding* to feeling unsafe, your reactive *behavior* is now unsafe for your relationship and for your partner.

It takes a lot of self-awareness to "press the pause button" and acknowledge that underneath the anger, there were initially more vulnerable emotions here, such as fear. And there are a lot of fears that can come up during interactions with your partner: fear that your partner doesn't care about you or your feelings, that you may lose them and end up alone, that you're not good enough for them, that you're not accepted for who you are—the list goes on and on. The antidote to your underlying fear is receiving the three elements of A.R.E. from your partner and giving them in return. This comforts our underlying insecurity, thus softening our reactivity.

The body responds in various ways to fear, such as increased heart rate, sweaty palms, and nervousness in the stomach. The body is literally impacted mentally, emotionally, and physically during conflict. American neurologist and physiologist Walter Bradford Cannon (1932) found that during distress, the homeostasis of our bodies changes, such as in blood flow and appetite. Homeostasis is the goal for most of us—it's when our bodies feel stabilized, in alignment, cool, calm, and collected. Those who have survived past traumas or difficult life experiences are quicker to fall out of homeostasis and into an automatic reaction mode because their fight-or-flight response button is more easily triggered by stress. This is the body's way of protecting itself to ensure that the bad thing doesn't happen again.

Think of the body's reaction as a super-sensitive fire alarm system that sometimes goes off incorrectly when it detects *any* sign of trouble. At first, it goes off only in response to real danger, which is helpful in appropriate circumstances. But eventually, the faulty alarm starts going off for no real reason when you're just trying to cook an omelet on a Sunday morning. This is frustrating and also confusing for the body. Is there real danger? Or can we just switch the alarm off and continue cooking the omelet? Relationship situations can feel similar: if either or both partners have had a lot of life experiences that taught the body to activate its internal alarm system often, that person is going to quickly retreat to fight-or-flight mode even when there's no real danger present.

EFT focuses on helping couples identify what is underneath these quick body reactions during fights—the deep, core vulnerable emotions and attachment needs. As therapists, we help our couples press the pause button, explore what they are thinking and feeling more deeply, and talk to each other about their vulnerable emotions, because this soft vulnerability (and responding to it) is what helps create a secure attachment in relationships. It looks like this: each partner has the experience of "My feelings matter to you, you are there for me, and you will show up for me" (in other words, A.R.E.). We help our couples learn to have internal insight and then share with their partners what's really going on for them—that initial fear underlying an episode of conflict—rather than instinctively reacting with anger, as we're all so inclined to do. The more couples can speak in a nonthreatening, nonreactive way, the safer it is for the partners to stick around, understand what's going on, and have empathy for each other.

EXERCISE: Testing Your Internal Alarm System

In your journal, explore the following:

- ◐ What initial fight-or-flight quick body reactions do you typically have in response to fearful situations?

- ◐ What initial fight-or-flight quick body reactions do you typically have in response to the emotion of fear in conflict situations with your partner?

- ◐ What does homeostasis feel like for you? How often are you in this stable, balanced state?

- ◐ How accurate is your internal "fire alarm" at detecting danger in your relationship? In what ways has it helped you? In what ways has it been frustrating for you?

Tying It All Together

Ultimately, the goal of EFT is to get to a place of secure attachment with your partner. This means learning how to be accessible, responsive, and engaged with them, and also creating a new pattern of interaction with them that is reciprocal and positive—even during the toughest times. Accomplishing these goals can be very difficult to do when our bodies and brains are primed to be reactive to conflict, especially when past events and experiences have trained our internal alarms systems to go off immediately. This is where learning how to cool off can be pivotal in your relationship, the subject of the next chapter.

CHAPTER 3

Cooling Down

Maria's fifteen-year marriage is hanging on by a thread. Fights heat up fast, with curse words flying all around and common occurrences of intentional hitting below the belt. One night, Maria's husband left after an argument and (unbeknownst to her) stayed at a hotel. She couldn't sleep without him; she was worried about his safety, angry he'd abandoned ship, and fearful it was the end. She messaged him for confirmation that he was safe but got no response, so she called. When he picked up the phone, she was instantly relieved to learn he was safe, but then just as quickly, a rush of rage slammed into her because she had been in so much turmoil. She told him to you-know-what, then hung up on him. He didn't get to hear about her fears for him and the relationship. He simply got verbally punched in the face.

As you can see with Maria, emotions run quick and fast during heated moments with our significant others. So this chapter is all about simmering down and finding new ways to react during those knee-jerk, fight-or-flight episodes. You'll learn how to become accountable for your own actions—on your side of the street—and decrease the chances of providing your partner with ammunition to be used against you.

Imagine having a toolbox, and each tool inside has a specific use. Some devices, such as a hammer, can be used in different ways and for different needs, such as pounding, pulling nails, and shaping metal. It can also be quite ineffective in some situations, such as when trying to insert a screw or sand down a surface. Similarly, each relationship tool has a time and place for helping you fix a problem or improve a situation. This is exactly what we will help you assemble in this chapter: a toolbox filled with tools for varying emotional situations. Some tools have multiple purposes, and others have a very specific use.

The overall goal is for you to be successful in your reactions by navigating your own emotional distress, thereby setting you up to better resolve conflicts. We are going to help you understand exactly why things get heated quickly, then provide specific steps you can take to calm your body down *and* help calm down your partner. We'll offer some "quick fixes" to help you put the fire out and de-escalate the conflict *fast*.

Why is this important? Because calming things down—in both your nervous system and the relationship—is a necessary step in changing the dynamic with your partner. Ultimately, you're working toward creating new opportunities to get your needs met. You may have noticed that trying over and over again to get your needs met during conflict just isn't working; that's why you have to try something different, turning the heat way down, in order to bring you two closer together.

The Role of Emotions in Conflict

Before we can talk about how to tamp the fires of conflict, we have to understand the kindling that fuels the fires: emotions and attachment needs. We all have the exact same buffet of emotions, and we are constantly exposed to them. Simply remembering a moment in your past, even subconsciously, can trigger a variety of emotional responses and can sometimes even feel as if the event were still happening now. Emotions are an important part of the authenticity that makes us who we are and they help us connect to our lives, to our surroundings, to others, and especially to ourselves.

Emotions are like a compass: they can help guide you by pointing you in the direction of your authenticity, values, beliefs, and needs. They help you understand what you are experiencing, assess whether it's good or bad, and determine what needs to change or what to do. Healthy emotional intelligence allows you to feel your emotions, name them, and sufficiently tolerate them (through coping) so you can make a good decision about what to do with them. So our aim here is to get you in charge of your emotions, rather than having them be in charge of you.

You may have spent the better part of your life avoiding hard emotions, positive emotions, or emotions altogether. But emotions aren't just intangible feelings that make us blow snot into tissues or punch walls. Emotions are neuropsychological states influenced by thoughts, behaviors, environment, mood, temperament, personality, and attachment histories—they can be very complex! At some points in the past, psychological practitioners have held that we and we alone are in control of our emotions, that others cannot or should not impact them; however, based on what we now know about human hardwiring, that's just plain wrong: you are *absolutely* emotionally impacted by others, as well by how you perceive a situation and by your past experiences. When your partner doesn't respond to you at all or forgets to put the cap on the toothpaste for the umpteenth time, having a negative emotional reaction is, well, normal.

Think back to a recent fight you had with your partner. What feelings did you have? Most people can immediately recall frustration, anger, anxiety, annoyance, or resentment. But what about the softer, more tender emotions under that—perhaps sadness—that are more challenging to detect? It's uncomfortable to stay in that place of vulnerability, like Maria, who couldn't stay in her fear and thus exploded. With EFT, we view emotions in two categories: primary emotions (the more tender and vulnerable ones that are *really* at play) and secondary emotions (the reactionary ones). This distinction is going to help you identify which tool to use in which situation.

First Things First: Primary Emotions

Primary emotions are called such because they come first: they are the initial feelings in response to an event. They are the raw, deeper emotions that instinctually draw people close. In the previous example, Maria's primary emotion was fear; she was afraid of losing her marriage and afraid for her husband's safety. Primary emotions show up as sensations within the body: heaviness in the chest and shoulders when sad, a knot in the stomach when scared, a tight queasiness when disgusted. Although you may not be aware of your primary emotions, everyone feels them.

Other examples of primary emotions include joy, loneliness, grief, hurt, longing, and excitement. They can be easy emotions or difficult emotions, but there is no such thing as a "bad" emotion. Rather, emotional responses arise either from feeling extremely connected and secure in a relationship (such as happiness, joy) or from feeling insecure and disconnected in a relationship (fear, loneliness). These are your core and authentic responses to a situation, and they act as that guiding compass toward your needs.

They will also, on an instinctive level, draw your partner closer to you, as they are much softer than secondary emotions. If you see a person yelling (driven by the secondary emotion of anger), you will naturally back away from them. If you see a person crying (primary emotion of sadness), you will naturally want to lean in and comfort them. This is our natural, hardwired way of relating to primary and secondary emotions. You can use this to your advantage in your relationship by focusing on showing your partner your more vulnerable primary emotions to create opportunities for more connectedness in times of need. The key is to slow down and listen.

Secondary Emotions

At times, it can be extremely challenging to slow down and notice our primary emotions. Sometimes we can't even find them at all! Instead, folks tend to get caught up in reactionary emotions—the secondary emotions that come after, in response to, the primary emotions. Secondary emotions get a lot more airtime because they're not as threatening for people, they're more protective. Couples find it easier to yell louder and express things with more intensity in an attempt to be understood (gain closeness) or to shut down discussions (to protect the relationship) than to risk being vulnerable by sharing their deeper primary emotions. But secondary emotions tend to push people away. Maria attempted to let her husband know she was not okay with his absence, but it backfired—because she resorted to her secondary emotions out of self-protection.

Common secondary emotions include anxiety, resentment, annoyance, frustration, apathy, anger, and a whole lot more like these. Sure, there are exceptions to the rule—as when anger is the appropriate primary emotion in the face of an extreme violation—but as a rule, these types of feelings are just masking what's underneath. We're quick to embrace secondary emotions because we think they shield us from vulnerability, but they're really just (at times subconscious) attempts to cope with the primary emotions we are feeling.

Primary Emotions	Secondary Emotions
Deeper and more vulnerable emotions, direct and authentic responses	*Reactive emotions, typically masking primary emotions*
• Joy/Excitement	• Anger/Frustration
• Hurt/Sadness	• Jealousy
• Sexual excitement	• Guilt
• Fear	• Resentment
• Love	• Anxiety
• Loneliness	• Shame/Self-blame

Primary and Secondary Emotions in Action

Let's return to Maria to show how primary and secondary emotions often show up in significant relationships. She was raised in a high-conflict, unpredictable, and physically dangerous home. Sharing any vulnerable (primary) emotions, such as fear or sadness, was just way too dangerous. She was often put down, abused, or physically hurt. She left home at sixteen and learned to take care of herself. Intensity and rage (secondary emotions) helped protect her. To this day, her autopilot response is to bypass her primary emotions and instead express herself from the more guarded place of her secondary emotions.

Because of this, her husband never really gets to experience her vulnerability—he doesn't know how much he matters to her or how worried she gets about losing him during their fights. Instead, she screams and curses at him, which teaches him that it's unsafe to get close to her. To protect his own hurt feelings, he hits back with criticism, horrible words, and put-downs. Thus, her fears are reinforced: *See? I can never show him my vulnerable parts.* Round and round they go.

So what's the problem with secondary emotions?

1. They push our partners away from us.

2. They don't get to the root of issues.

3. Because they aren't primary, deep, core emotions, they aren't identifying our real attachment needs, which will help us solve the problem.

And why should we prioritize primary emotions?

1. They instinctively draw our partners closer to us.

2. They get to the root of issues quicker.

3. They help us problem solve faster.

One great thing about accessing primary emotions is that once they are felt and experienced, you can move through them and on from them. With secondary emotions, on the other hand, you can get stuck in them because they're not an accurate representation of what's really going on. This makes them cause discomfort and disconnection for longer periods of time.

Maria and her husband have a lot of work to do to reestablish safety and stop reacting on autopilot. In order to salvage the relationship, they'll need to take a deep dive into what is really going on underneath their reactionary behaviors so they can connect around their mutual needs more effectively.

Sandra and Zahir's Story

Sandra and Zahir haven't had sex in ten years. Without realizing it at all, they've been stuck in their secondary emotions: Zahir feeling angry and bitter toward his wife, Sandra feeling resentful and annoyed at Zahir's attempts to initiate sex with her when she isn't feeling close to him. Throughout the years, an extreme sense of rejection has built up in Zahir—he misses feeling desired by his wife and fears she'll never want him again, which only leads to further disconnection.

At the same time, Sandra feels unseen and alone in the marriage. She believes her husband only wants sex to get his physical needs met, he doesn't want her. This leaves her feeling both emotionally and sexually disconnected from him, which is both painful and scary for her. If he doesn't actually want her, can't he easily go elsewhere to get his sexual needs met?

In counseling, this couple is led to uncover the primary emotions they've both been avoiding and feeling—their sadness and hurt at the disconnection between them, and also the fear they both have that their relationship is totally unraveling. But once they become aware of the underlying emotions causing them to react the way they have been, they're able to start taming the fires of conflict that often rage between them. By identifying the deep primary emotions underneath their secondary emotions and learning to cope with them, the couple is then able to explore their attachment needs and allow a new dynamic to unfold.

TOOLS FOR YOUR TOOLBOX:
What to Do with Emotions

Here's a three-step process for dealing with your emotions when they're in control of you instead of vice versa.

Step 1: Pay Attention

When in conflict, your primary emotions act as a signal to what is important to you at that moment—a deep need. Unfortunately, our secondary emotions take over fast. All primary emotions live in the body as physical sensations. When you make a habit of pressing the pause button and paying attention to your physical feelings, you can learn to identify your deeper emotions and their importance. Taking a deep breath gives you a few extra seconds to do this before responding, before adding kindling to the fire.

If you are angry, there must be deeper emotions going on. You are upset about something that matters to you. The key to changing your reactions is to slow things down, identify which emotion is tied to which sensation, and figure out your more vulnerable feelings. Your body will tell you first by having a physical reaction—so pay attention. When you start to feel an emotion, focus on where you physically feel it in your body. Do a head-to-toe survey of where you identify lightness, tension, tightness, sinking of the stomach, or relief.

Then try to sift through any secondary emotions that may be getting in the way of what's really bothering you. Secondary emotions can be felt in the body as well, they just feel different than primary emotions. Perhaps you're so frustrated that you feel shaky. That's okay, that's normal. Take a breath and sit with that. But then take another deep breath and explore further: Is there another sensation underneath the jittery frustration? It's common for there to be layers to physical emotional experiences.

This may be difficult and awkward at first, but with time, you'll be able to naturally get in touch with your genuine emotions and how they feel in your body. Learning how to actually feel our feelings calms our bodies and our emotions down, so it's a great first step in putting out your own fires. When you do this, it will lead to your partner to respond differently too.

Step 2: Name It

Now stay with the feeling in your body for a moment; focus on that tightness in your neck, the giddy energy in your feet, or your sweaty palms. If you move on too soon, you'll suppress the emotion, which isn't what we want, because ignored emotions often continue to manifest in larger ways.

Walk yourself through the emotion. *What am I feeling? Why am I feeling this way?* Try hard to identify the primary emotion at work and put a name to it. If you aren't able to identify it and instead come up with naming a secondary emotion (like anger), that's okay. Great job noticing! Work toward naming that emotion first, as research shows that putting words to our emotional experiences helps calm us (which in turn will calm the fire you're experiencing with your partner). Make sure you give yourself time to sit with the named emotion before you take further action, if needed. Don't try to move past the emotion before you're ready, before you've come to a place of experiencing it and naming it.

Step 3: Apply What You Discover

The primary emotion(s) you identified will point you to what's really going on inside you, so you can communicate in a way that impacts how your partner will respond. For example, if Maria had been in touch with her primary emotions before calling her husband, she could have said, "Thank you for answering the phone. We are both upset from our fighting. I am relieved to know you are okay, and I am feeling really scared of losing you. Let's talk tomorrow when you are home." In doing so, she would be acknowledging her relief, recognizing the conflict, and also sharing her fear. This is what it looks like to apply the recognition of primary emotions.

EXERCISE: Identify and Reflect on Your Primary and Secondary Emotions

Now it's your turn to identify and reflect on your primary and secondary emotions. Think back to a recent conflict with your partner. Allow yourself to reenter the situation. Pull out your journal and answer these prompts:

- What message did you get about yourself and/or the relationship?

- What secondary emotion(s) did you feel?

- What primary emotion(s) did you feel?

- What were your attachment needs?

- How did you try to draw your partner close to you, if at all?

- How did you push your partner away from you, if at all?

- What would you have needed to feel better, to feel as if the issue were resolved?

- In general, when things escalate in your relationship, what secondary emotion do you typically go to?

- What are the typical primary emotions underneath this that you notice?

Incorporating Attachment Needs with Emotions

Many people struggle with identifying what they feel, and therefore, they have no clue what they may really and truly need from their partner. This goes far beyond feeling like you "just *need* him to do the dishes" or "just *need* her to have more sex with me." We're talking about those deep, core attachment needs (also referred to as "emotional needs") we've been focusing on. And this is super important in relationships, because we can't expect our partners to know what we need if we don't know what we are feeling and craving in moments of conflict. Read that one again—that's how important it is: *Your partner can't read your mind and won't be able to tell what you are feeling and what you are needing unless you tell them.*

Remember, our core, primary emotions form our body's compass, guiding us toward our authenticity and our attachment needs. A great example of this is hunger. Hunger is something you feel in your body, just like an emotion, that alerts your brain to a need: a need for food. Similarly, it is important for you to fully understand your emotions and what is going on inside your body on an emotional level because the quicker you know what you are feeling, the easier it will be for you to name your emotion, cope with it, and then identify the thing that will be a game changer for your relationship: you will be able to identify your *attachment needs.*

By now, you are aware that underneath the less helpful behaviors in your conflict interaction with your partner are the juicy, vulnerable primary emotions. When couples feel disconnected and insecure in the relationship, their safety and closeness are threatened. Here is where the change comes in: you get to start figuring out what attachment needs you have by using your primary emotions.

Believe it or not, you may need something more from your partner than just hearing you are right (although that can feel good at times). We all want to be right, but there is more to it, and this is where your attachment needs come in. Here's an example: Think about a time when you continued to explain yourself over and over again during a disagreement with your partner, but you just didn't feel you were getting anywhere. So you started to increase your volume, and before you knew it, you were yelling to get your point across. What was happening here was that you weren't feeling heard.

When we continuously try to explain our position, it is usually because, underneath, we are scared that we aren't being heard, that what we have to say doesn't matter to the person who matters most to us. The underlying attachment need here is to be seen, to be understood, and to feel that what you have to say *matters* to them. This is the core, underlying attachment need—and as you can see, it isn't really about your partner taking out the garbage or coming home late. It's something deeper and more vulnerable: it's about a primary, core emotion.

Fights can be confusing because they tend to be focused on a topic—such as the content in your life, like pets, household chores, parenting, past hurts, and so forth—but really, the energy behind fights is more about *underlying primary emotions* and core, vulnerable *emotional attachment needs*. We need something from our partner, but we might not be saying it clearly. It gets lost in translation, especially when we don't identify our primary emotions first.

Here are some emotional needs in the relationship that partners are often asking for (either indirectly or directly) during a fight:

- To be seen

- To feel/be safe

- To know that your emotions matter

- To feel loved

- To be protected

- To feel wanted and appreciated

- To feel sexually desired

- To feel good enough

- To belong

- To feel as if what matters to you matters to your partner

Identifying these needs can be a helpful tool in cooling down conflict because it points you in the direction of how to cope with uncomfortable emotions when they arise. People often ask for their needs to be met without vulnerability, and unfortunately, it comes out as criticism every time. Eventually, you'll learn how to share the needs that will draw your partner closer to you and discuss them together, but we aren't quite there yet. For now, let's keep working on putting out the fires of conflict in your relationship with a handful of exercises.

Five Exercises for Five Common Attachment Fears

Here are five typical attachment-related fears that often cause problems in romantic relationships:

1. Fear of abandonment

2. Fear of rejection

3. Fear of not being good enough

4. Fear of feelings not mattering

5. Fear of conflict

Which of these resonate with you the most? Return to the last exercise you did, when you identified your primary and secondary emotions around a recent conflict with your partner. Now in your journal, write down one to three deep-rooted emotional needs you had *during* the conflict, then write down what would have provided you comfort *at that moment.* These insights will come in handy as we proceed through the corresponding exercises you can try the next time each particular attachment-related fear arises.

EXERCISE: Fear of Abandonment

Get out a good old-fashioned shoebox, the kind you used to keep your mementos in when you were younger. We're going to create a love box! Next, gather up all the cards, letters, and items that remind you of the love your partner has for you and put them in this box. If most of your reminders are digital, contained in text messages or emails, take screenshots of the snippets that represent your love and print them out (or you can create your love box in the form of a folder on your computer or phone instead).

Each time you fear that your partner will abandon you, go through your love box, reading every word they wrote you and handling every trinket you've collected throughout your romance together. While taking deep breaths, remind yourself that you are safe, that your partner still loves you, even during conflict. The trick here is remembering to go to your love box when your abandonment fear is triggered.

EXERCISE: Fear of Rejection

Any type of rejection—from a lover or from a job application—is painful. Rejection is encoded in the same part of the brain as physical pain, so when we say that rejection is painful, we really mean it. When you're feeling rejected, assure yourself that your pain is real, allow yourself to feel it, and remind yourself that the pain will pass through you. Don't jump into reaction/retaliation mode and don't try to shove down or numb the pain with alcohol, drugs, shopping, or food. Painful emotions are safe and they are okay.

Can you think of moments when your partner did not reject you and did reach for you? Maybe not in the exact way that you're hoping for now, but any moment, however small, is important to notice. Maybe they recently rejected your sexual advances but they've been asking to plan a date night or have been cooking your favorite meal. Start a list of the times your partner has reached for you and continues to reach for you, and read it over whenever your fear of rejection surfaces. Taking deep breaths, remind yourself of all the ways your partner *does* want you and *does* attempt to connect with you, even if it's not in the ways you've been looking for at this time.

EXERCISE: Fear of Not Being Good Enough

People can drown in the sense of not being enough for their partners when it seems like all they're hearing from them is how they're getting it wrong, when they're given explanation after explanation about how they're missing the mark. Some partners struggle with blaming, commonly employing all-or-nothing language like, "You *never* ..." and "You *always* ..."

When this feeling of not being good enough washes over you, remind yourself of this fact: this isn't the message your partner is trying to send.

They're actually trying to reach for you, but their intent is getting lost in the translation of their own secondary emotions and lack of communication skills. You actually *are* enough for them, and they're fighting to be seen by *you* precisely *because* you *are* enough. You matter to them. They aren't reaching for someone else. So tell yourself that everything is going to be okay. You are good enough, even when your partner is upset with you. Your partner's blame game and black-or-white language isn't about being wrong or right, so you don't have to play along by proving the fact that you actually *did* do the laundry.

In your journal, write down five things you do or have done in your life that remind you that you are enough exactly as you are, not defined by the viewpoint of your partner. Read this list over and over again when you doubt your self-worth. Adopt a mantra you can repeat while taking deep breaths: "It is okay for me to be okay while my partner is not okay. My partner's distress or view of me does not define who I am." Keep saying it, until the truth of it sinks in.

EXERCISE: Fear of Feelings Not Mattering

Feeling emotionally seen and heard by our partner lies at the core of connection, and when we get the message that our feelings don't matter, it can be painful as well as triggering—it can bring up memories from the past when you got this message from others.

Not only will you have to work hard at pressing the pause button to calm yourself down when this fear rears its ugly head, but you will also need to be your own coach here. Your job is to assure yourself that your emotions *do* matter—your partner is just having a hard time showing it at the moment. Don't internalize that! Don't dismiss your own emotions. Instead, whenever someone you care about deeply is not validating your emotions, validate your feelings yourself. Literally tell yourself, "I feel this way, and that makes sense and is okay. My feelings are valid."

EXERCISE: Fear of Conflict

We all hate conflict, but there's another way of looking at it: conflict is actually a means of couples *fighting for the relationship*. The end goal for them here is to get connected. We know that sounds crazy, because when conflict arises, it doesn't feel at all like a pathway to something positive. But it is and it can be.

So give yourself another mantra to calm yourself when fights erupt. Taking deep breaths, repeat over and over: "Conflict is a way my partner is reaching for closeness; my partner is fighting for me because I matter to them. I am safe. It is safe for me to be in conflict. We can stop at any point."

Emotional Regulation

We've regularly been using terms like "the need to cool off" and "control your side of the street." Language such as this refers to regulating your emotions, and if you don't have much experience in this department—if you feel your emotions tend to control you far more than you control them—it's helpful to be aware of some foundational emotional regulation concepts.

Basically, when our emotions get the best of us and feel intolerable, one of two things happens: we move into a state of hyperarousal or we move into a state of hypoarousal.

Hyperarousal is a state of physical activation—it's the state that elicits the fight-or-flight automatic reaction mode, and in this state, emotions feel intense, whether that's anger, panic, fear, hypervigilance, anxiety, or, at its worst, rage and hostility (Roe n.d.). In hyperarousal, you feel out of control, emotionally flooded, and overwhelmed. It's almost like your body has gotten away from you and is spinning out—our energy can get stuck there, in that state of activation. You know how we talked about going from zero to sixty in a flash earlier in the book? Well, that's one indicator of hyperarousal—within seconds, you want to throw things and cuss out your partner. Your heart races, you're impulsive, and it's hard to slow down in this state.

Hypoarousal is a state of underactivation. This is the default setting for some people when emotions feel too big for what the brain and body are able to tolerate. As a result, it's like the body's light switch just goes "off" … and stays there. You may notice feelings of disconnection, apathy, exhaustion, depression, fatigue—you feel spaced out, zoned out, or numb (Roe n.d.). Your emotions and energy level likely feel "flat."

Knowing which state you are in can help you determine which of the two tools below to reach for in your toolbox.

TOOLS FOR YOUR TOOLBOX:
How to Regulate During Hyperarousal

- **Call it out:** Take away the power of hyperarousal simply by acknowledging that you are in this overactive state.

- **Gauge your own emotions:** Measure your frustration level on a scale of 0 to 10. Acknowledge your agitation to yourself. When possible, inform your partner if your number is high; let them know you need to cool down in order to move forward in the conversation.

- **Do deep tummy breathing:** Breathe in through your nose and out through your mouth. Double the length of your exhales (for example, breathe in for five seconds, out for ten) to activate the part of your brain that calms.

- **Take a negotiated break:** If you're having trouble calming down, step away from the interaction for a minimum of twenty to thirty minutes (the time it takes to regulate)—longer if you have a trauma history—before coming back to the conversation.

- **Use mindfulness:** Increase your awareness of your body sensations. Do not react, act out, or make judgments; just notice the sensations and breathe through them.

- **Use smell:** Scents such as lavender are known to have a calming effect.

- **Journal:** Emotionally dump out what you're feeling on the page. Be frustrated on paper, not in person. Then rationally organize your thoughts and share them with your partner when you are ready.

- **Change your body temperature:** Take a cold shower, drink cold water, put an ice pack on your body. This is a way to shock your body back to normal without going into self-harm or making unhealthy or impulsive decisions.

- **Use affirmations:** Talk yourself down: "Emotions are okay. It is okay for me to feel bad, it will pass. It is okay for my partner to feel bad, it will pass."

- **Twist:** While sitting, twist the top half of your body from left to right from the shoulders. This helps activate the part of the nervous system that calms us down.

- **Label:** Identify the emotion in your body and give it a name.

- **Do a HALT self-check:** Are you hungry, angry, lonely, or tired? These are common distress triggers. Sleep, nutrition, and social connections will all help you regulate.

- **Meditate:** This practice helps you return to your baseline. You can use an app like Calm or Insight Timer.

- **Play music:** Play calming, soothing music you like, focusing on the rhythms, beats, and lyrics.

- **Eat comfort food:** Reach for something nostalgic that's always provided comfort. Your brain releases serotonin (the happy hormone) when eating.

- **Drink warm water:** Swallowing warm water, tea, or coffee helps regulate the body.

- **Get the energy out:** Shake, stomp, or brush off the agitating energy from your body.

- **Put your legs up:** Lie on your back with your legs in the air perpendicular to your body, or lie on your back with your rear against a wall, your legs straight up the wall for support. This helps activate the part of your brain that calms.

TOOLS FOR YOUR TOOLBOX:
How to Regulate During Hypoarousal

- **Call it out:** Take away the power of hypoarousal simply by acknowledging that you are in this understimulated state.

- **Use movement:** Stand up, stretch, take a walk, jump on a trampoline, do a cartwheel.

- **Connect to music:** Dance, sing, or listen to emotionally evocative music.

- **Use art:** Draw, paint, doodle.

- **Ground yourself:** Fight dissociation by bringing your body back to the here-and-now present moment: put your feet flat on the floor, notice the space around you, name five things you can see, four things you can touch, three things you can hear, and two things you can smell.

- **Eat:** Consume something interesting that engages your senses, like something crunchy or fragrant.

- **Use scents:** Put your sense of smell to work with invigorating odors like citrus and peppermint.

- **Meditate:** Come back into the present moment by following a guided meditation on YouTube or through your favorite app.

- **Increase your heart rate:** Do some cardio exercise, like running up and down the street.

- **Do a HALT self-check:** Are you hungry, angry, lonely, or tired? If so, what act of self-care can you engage in to regulate?

- **Use touch:** Play with something tactile, such as a fidget spinner or an interesting-feeling object.

- **Gain awareness:** Pause to give yourself time to be curious about what emotion is driving your reactions. What was happening right before you began to shut down? What were you feeling, thinking, or doing?

- **Rock:** Simulate a rocking motion—in a rocking chair, on a regular chair or yoga ball, curled up on the floor in a ball.

Finding an Emotional Middle Ground

In our relationships, rather than being stuck in hyperarousal or hypoarousal, we want to be in what is called a "window of tolerance" with our emotions. This is where the distress is not gone but is tolerable enough for you to engage with it. It doesn't drown either you or your partner. Like Goldilocks, you're looking for that "just right" feeling that is neither "too hot" nor "too cold." So if you notice yourself slipping into hypo- or hyperarousal, use the strategies listed above. It can be helpful to remind yourself that all emotions are temporary: no matter how big or how painful, whether primary or secondary, they will eventually pass.

In a heated interaction with your partner, it's reasonable to find yourself wanting to disengage from the conflict either by freezing, fleeing, appeasing, or fighting. You may find yourself yelling or intimidating your partner to get them to stop whatever is triggering you. Or you might shut down, withdraw, pacify, or just up and leave to get the conflict to stop. We all have patterns we fall into—not just you, but your partner as well.

But once you learn to regulate your emotional patterns of hyper- or hypoarousal—once you can get yourself in a space where your emotions are tolerable and you are within your window of tolerance—that's the green light to proceed. That's the "just right" place. Great job!

EXERCISE: The Skill of Deep Breathing

Why the heck does everyone talk so much about the simple act of breathing as a coping skill? When you're in a state of distress, deep breathing, after all, feels very far removed and is the last thing on your mind. But get this: deep breathing can activate the parasympathetic nervous system by essentially tricking your brain into thinking you're calmer than you're feeling. Essentially, your brain registers your slow, measured breathing and says to itself, *I can't actually be in danger right now because clearly I am deep breathing. This wouldn't be physically possible if I were truly in danger, so I must be safe. I can calm down now.* And voilà! Suddenly, your brain sends your body cues to calm down and functioning goes back to normal. It's like magic!

The next time you are in conflict and need to reach for a coping skill, try this one first:

1. Rate the level of your distress on a scale from 0 to 10 (where 0 is the lowest and 10 is the highest).

2. Now try something called "box breathing," which follows a pattern:

   ● Breathe in through your nose for five seconds.

   ● Hold at the top for five seconds.

   ● Breathe out through your mouth for five seconds.

   ● Hold at the bottom for five seconds.

   You end up tracing around the outside of a box, like this:

3. Do this breathing technique three to five times.

4. Now rate your distress level again on the same scale of 0 to 10. Did your number change?

Note: Notice how the box breathing technique works for you with five-second intervals and feel free to adjust the number of seconds up or down based on the unique needs of your own body.

Intense Emotional Pain

Does it feel at times like the fighting with your partner is so severe that you'd rather experience physical pain than emotional pain? Or do either one of you ever end up threatening self-harm? Some people feel emotions so deeply that it is difficult for them to function. Usually, the pain comes from the experience of abandonment, of feeling as if they don't matter. Because of our deep, ingrained need for human connectedness, this pain can feel unbearable and can lead to self-harm in an attempt to stop the emotional pain by making it physical instead, which seems more manageable.

This coping strategy of self-harm can be very dangerous and cause more problems. First of all, you are hurting yourself. Second, your partner will become more fearful in the relationship, scared that you will hurt yourself and scared to share how they feel for fear of setting you off, which will create even more distance and distress between the two of you. Using self-harm as a cry for help during scary times makes things worse.

It's like being stuck in quicksand. It's terrifying to feel yourself gradually sinking, but the quicker you move, the quicker you sink more. Similarly, the more terrified you are about losing your relationship and experiencing feelings of division while threatening or engaging in self-harm, the worse things will get. That's why the healthy regulation strategies we've been presenting in this chapter are so vital to reducing harm during times of intense distress.

If you find yourself self-harming, or threatening to harm yourself during conflicts with your partner, you should reach out for professional therapeutic support as soon as possible. Crisis lines can be a great resource in these moments, like the Crisis Lifeline at 1-800-273-8255 (or its simpler 988 code) for those in the United States. Or you can text "HOME" to 741741 to immediately connect via text message with a crisis counselor. And if you are ever worried for your own or your partner's safety, *always, always, always* call 911. The purpose of these resources is to help you manage the pain and distress *by not having to manage them alone*. Remember:

You are not alone. You are never alone. Painful feelings are temporary. There are tools and options available to help you navigate difficult waters.

When It's Not You, It's Them

We are now going to the other side of the spectrum, when the madness has nothing to do with you and everything to do with them. In some relationships, responsibility for the conflicts really isn't a two-way street. In some relationships, it really is just one of the partners who is simply out of control, acting crazy, and making irrational decisions that are very damaging. These are the individuals who are extremely difficult, who gaslight their mates, and who are rageful. Their words and their behaviors do not match. Their blow-ups are unpredictable, harsh, and extreme. The partners of such individuals try all kinds of techniques to manage the relationship difficulties, but they're just not effective. They may learn to fight back just to survive in the relationship, but without their partner's cooperation and participation in making things better, there's little they can do on their own. But that doesn't mean there's little they can do for *themselves.*

You may be caught in this kind of tough situation. You love your partner, but you also know their behaviors are toxic, eroding away at your bond, and making you feel emotionally unsafe. Your partner may be threatening their life (or yours), manipulating you, or sabotaging the relationship—you should know that these dangerous behaviors are not normal in relationships. So what can you do?

First, focus on empowering yourself, taking care of yourself, seeking out a therapist, and knowing your self-worth. It is never okay for anyone to be or to feel trapped in a toxic dynamic.

Second, set boundaries with your partner using the method presented in chapter 1. This gives them a chance to change, and if they don't, it gives you a chance to consider whether this relationship is the right choice or not. Follow through on your boundaries—assume they will try to cross them over and over, so you will need to hold strong.

Third, focus on building your support system. Talk with your "green light" people (even if you feel embarrassed or ashamed) and do a reality check with them. Your community will help empower you. Don't continue the cycle of gaslighting you may have experienced by doubting yourself and your reality. In these types of relationships, it is common for these partners to *not* read self-help books like you're doing, to *not* participate with you in therapeutic solutions. In such cases, your job here is to learn, grow, and make a better life for *yourself*, which may include exiting the toxic relationship.

Quick Reference: Your Conflict Toolbox

Before we conclude this chapter's discussion of cooling down in heated times, we want to offer a handy tool, a "cheat sheet," that you can easily reference when you start to notice the signs and symptoms of emotional distress and conflict cropping up in your relationship interactions. This is a cumulation of many of the situations we reviewed in this chapter, reminding you what they look like and what you can do in the face of them.

Many of our clients stick a printed version of this on the fridge, because the kitchen seems to be a common area for conflicts to arise. (As such, we've made this tool available as a downloadable PDF at http://www .newharbinger.com/51932, where you can also find the "11 Facts About Emotions to Cool Conflict" resource, relevant to this chapter's content as well.) Wherever you choose to store this information, make sure it's a central location, in an easy-to-notice place, so that you and your partner can start regularly practicing these methods to break harmful and hurtful patterns and build new ones together.

CONFLICT TOOLBOX

What You Notice	What to Do
Frustration or anger at your partner	1. Press the pause button. 2. Take a deep breath. 3. Find a vulnerable, primary emotion underneath (are you hurt, scared, sad, lonely?).
A primary emotion toward your partner	1. Sit with it! 2. Feel it in your body. 3. Stay within your window of tolerance. 4. Once the emotion is processed, identify what attachment needs are involved and decide what to do next.
Desire to share a feeling with your partner	Make sure you share only primary emotions—the secondary ones will keep your negative cycle going and push your partner farther away. Vulnerability draws closeness.
A vulnerable attachment need for your partner	Use one of the above exercises to cope with the pain of this attachment need while you and your partner are cooling off. Then share the need with them, combining a vulnerability with a need. Sharing a need without a vulnerability will sound critical.
Shame	1. Good people feel bad about doing bad things. Remind yourself you are a good person because you feel bad. 2. Fight the urge to not let your shame be in the driver's seat and take you offline from your partner. 3. Force yourself to regulate using the tools provided here, and stay online for your partner so you can stay connected.

What You Notice	What to Do
Feeling a big emotion that feels outside your window of tolerance	1. Press the pause button. Identify whether you are in hypoarousal or hyperarousal. 2. Use the coping tools provided in this chapter. 3. Once back in the window of tolerance, sit with the emotion and listen to it, experience it in your body, and practice with the tools in your growing toolbox.
Numbness or zoning out during conflict	Acknowledge that you are in hypoarousal and follow the procedures to regulate that state.
Extreme anxiety or feeling overwhelmed during conflict	Acknowledge that you are in hyperarousal and follow the procedures to regulate that state.
Desire to self-harm or threaten self-harm during conflict	1. Pause. Create safety for yourself right away (if you are in danger, call 911). 2. Reach out to a friend, crisis line, or your therapist for support. 3. Regulate your emotions using the healthy coping tools provided in this chapter. 4. Remind yourself that all emotions are temporary.
Desire to act on a secondary emotion or make an impulsive decision	Press the pause button. Identify the primary emotion underneath. Wait until your emotions are fully processed before making any decisions.

Tying It All Together

We covered a ton of information in this chapter about why things escalate and what you can do when that happens, with the goal of calming down distress so that you and your partner can get to a place of reconnection again. If it feels like a lot, that's because it is! But the more aware you are of what kindles the flames of your relationship conflict fires and the more you can learn how to tamp down those flames, the easier the tools, exercises, and techniques will become. Like anything else that starts off hard, it becomes easier with practice.

On the other hand, if you and your partner found success with the recommendations in this chapter, it's common to already feel better at this stage and think you've got things all figured out. But don't stop the work. Keep reading! The chapters that follow have more to offer in terms of getting to the root of your relationship issues and creating deeper, long-term change, as in the next chapter, where we turn to identifying the patterns and cycles that are maintaining the conflict in your relationship.

CHAPTER 4

Caught in the Cycle: Identifying the Pattern

You now understand more about why we act the way we do in relationships and why EFT is particularly effective for solving relational problems. You also have some helpful tools and tips under your belt now for how to calm down quickly and get some relief in intensely heated moments. So now you're probably wondering, *How do I stop the freakin' fights from happening in the first place?*

In high-conflict relationships, people tend to behave in ways they never thought they would, scream in ways they never thought they could, and find themselves in dynamics they never thought they'd tolerate. The hurts are so large, they feel impossible to get over. We're talking about the *cycle* of fighting, fighting, fighting that has invaded your relationship, and EFT is so helpful in this regard because it's focused on de-escalating the conflictual cycle. In turn, a new pathway toward secure attachment with your partner opens up. So you can think of this entire chapter as a guide for decreasing the intensity and frequency of your fighting and getting closer to the goal of secure attachment. In our ongoing metaphor of building your "dream home" with your partner, this chapter's content forms the walls and the structure of the whole house.

Now think back to your most recent argument with your partner. Was there a point at which you thought, *Why are we just going around and around in circles? Didn't I just say that same thing two minutes ago? Didn't they already tell me that? Why aren't they listening to me? Why are our fights always like this?*

If you find yourself with thoughts like this or getting that "uh-oh, here we go again" feeling in your gut whenever an argument starts ramping up, then you guessed it: you are trapped in a *negative cycle*. You're aware that you and your partner are about to take a turn from conversation into a big fight. Your alarms go off, and no matter how hard you try to stop the argument, things go into the ditch fast. Couples tend to know exactly who will do what and exactly what to expect during their fights—it's a predictable pattern. And most of the time, their predictions are right! One person blames and so the other gets defensive and shuts down. The more one shuts down, the more the other explains and gets louder. These cycles, or patterns, in couples cause a divide between them and deep attachment insecurities over time. They don't result in closer connections and a better understanding of each other.

Your negative cycle with your partner is a cascading pattern of actions and reactions that create the escalation between you. Your cycle is predictably consistent, and the two of you likely maintain similar behaviors each time your cycle is set in motion. The cycle becomes negative when you don't feel safe or secure with the interaction or an aspect of the relationship with your partner. And there's a domino effect to your cycle in that each person's behaviors and reactions influence the other person's behaviors and reactions. One partner makes a comment, the other makes another comment back. Soon, there is yelling and screaming, but underneath this seeming chaos lie those softer, deeper primary emotions we talked about in the last chapter and needs that aren't getting met or addressed. Because these primary emotions and needs aren't being talked about, it feels safer to just snap back and react from anger. Thus the negative cycle is perpetually sustained and escalation kicks into high gear.

Let's get one thing straight from the start: every couple has a negative cycle they fall into in times of stress. Yes, we really do mean *every* couple (even our own relationships!). But your negative cycle may feel so comfortable, so familiar, that you may not even notice you're in it until the fight is way far gone. Like a worn-in cushion or a groove in the mattress, you can't help but slide into that space, even if it's not the most pleasant place to be.

It's no different than any other bad habit, like drinking too much. One minute you feel fine, but the next you've slipped over into "one too many" territory because you stopped paying attention. Next thing you know, you might start saying things you didn't mean to say and you're not able to drive yourself home—you're too far gone. This is why empowering you with an understanding of negative cycles in relationships is a potent step in learning how stop your cycle.

We've said it before and we'll say it again: knowledge is power. You need to recognize that you are in a negative cycle so you don't get taken for a ride by it and can instead take control of the wheel yourself. In this chapter, we'll help you identify your own unique cycle with your partner and we'll teach you how to respond rather than react for immediate relief.

Playing Ping-Pong

Cause and effect is a fascinating and important concept to consider in relationships, because it's fair and reasonable to assume that any human is going to have a reaction to how any other human is acting toward them. As we talked about early in the book, we are bonding mammals, wired for connection with others even before birth. We are not "independent" from others (even if there's a part of you that wishes you were), we do not live in a vacuum uninfluenced by other people, and our brains are programmed to have responses and reactions to others.

So the communication cycle with your partner is like a ping-pong match. One of you serves, the other hits back in a particular way, the other has to respond (choosing not to keep playing, by the way, is still a response—and a big one, at that), and then the other hits back accordingly. We do this back-and-forth with our nonverbal cues, our words, our energy, our body language, everything—and each response can either escalate or de-escalate an interaction.

No matter how toxic your partner or relationship has become, your reaction can still have an influence. And while we don't want to be a negative Nelly here, *you* are part of how the system of your relationship moves into conflict as well. It takes two to tango, after all. Because you're part of the problem, it only stands to reason that you're part of the solution too. It's all in how you react to your partner's behaviors and emotions, and the ways in which you share your emotions and show your behaviors to them.

Here's a flow diagram that illustrates a typical ping-pong match between couples, so you can see cause-and-effect reciprocity in action:

Partner 1 (serves the ball; insert contemptuous tone here): "Are you *really* going out with your friends *again* tonight?" (*Poking, criticizing.*)

⇩

Partner 2 (hits ball back): "It's not a big deal. We spent *all day* together." (*Minimizing, invalidating, defensiveness.*)

⇩

Partner 1 (hits ball back): "Whatever. You don't even care about spending time with me. You probably don't even like me." (*Criticizing, blaming, accusing.*)

⇩

Partner 2 (hits ball back): "Are you kidding me? I'm so sick of your complaints. You're always like this. I need a break." (*Criticizing, withdrawing, threatening.*)

⇩

Partner 1 (doesn't hit the ball back): [Storms off to the other room.] (*Stonewalling, withdrawing.*)

⇩

Partner 2 (doesn't pick up the ball, doesn't try to keep the game going, flips the ping-pong table over): [Slams the door on the way out of the house for the night.] (*Stonewalling, withdrawing, reacting out of anger, getting "big."*)

Getting to the Root of Things

When therapists talk about getting to the root of things, they mean identifying the main issue(s) of a problem and then correcting it. That's what we work to do with our couples: fix the main problem hampering their growth.

Roots have an important function in plants: they're what grounds them, attaches them to the earth, and feeds them—their source of nutrients. In our daily lives, we don't see the intricacies of the roots—of a rose, for example. When you walk by, all you see is the top part of the flower, maybe some thorns as well.

Our human interactions are like this. On a day-to-day basis, we see only what's going on above the ground (behaviors/reactions and secondary emotions), not the below-the-ground roots (insecurities and underlying primary emotions and needs) that are actually feeding what we can witness. But it's these tender, more vulnerable roots that actually draw our partners close.

When in conflict, we show the rosebud in bloom (the big reactive behaviors) and the thorns (the prickly secondary emotions of anger and frustration), but the roots are hidden away. And yet it's the roots at the source that are actually fueling the entire interaction—our core insecurities and the softer primary emotions that represent our authentic selves. Couples typically don't express these softer emotions and needs in a clear way (as you saw above with partner 1 and partner 2), so communication becomes combative, sharing only the secondary emotions and reactionary behaviors.

To de-escalate the negative cycle in your relationship, you need to get to the root of the problem with your partner. This is what couples in secure attachment relationships can do quickly: get past the secondary emotions and big reactions as fast as possible and access the roots. When couples share their vulnerable primary feelings and attachment needs, change happens much more quickly!

Typical Attachment Style Reactions in a Negative Cycle

Here are a few examples of what's going on above and below the surface in many unhealthy relationship dynamics.

Anxious Attachment

Above the ground—what you see:

> *Behavior*: criticism, questioning, chasing, yelling, blaming, poking, nitpicking, banging on the car door while the other is driving away
>
> *Secondary emotion*: frustration, annoyance, anger, righteous indignation, anxiety, hyperarousal

Below the ground—what you don't see:

> *Primary emotion*: loneliness, fear of not mattering to one's partner, sadness, fear of abandonment
>
> *Underlying attachment need*: to feel seen, heard, loved, and important to partner

Avoidant Attachment

Above the ground—what you see:

> *Behavior:* shutting down, leaving, going quiet, looking at the phone, pacifying; not sharing feelings, needs, or opinions; having an "everything's fine" attitude; defending; eventually blowing up with yelling and name-calling

> *Secondary emotion:* frustration, annoyance, anger, defensiveness, anxiety, hyperarousal or hypoarousal

Below the ground—what you don't see:

> *Primary emotion:* fear of conflict, fear of losing partner, fear of not being good enough, sadness over disconnection, loneliness

> *Underlying attachment need:* to feel good enough, to feel accepted by partner, to feel safe in the conflict and in the relationship, to feel loved by partner

Understanding Your Insecurities

You've already learned that what lies at the root of relationship conflict is an insecure attachment bond (often arising from an "anxious" or "avoidant" attachment style and the negative cycle) and unmet attachment needs (like the emotional yearning for security). Attachment insecurities in relationships create relational fear and distress. As we saw in the verbal ping-pong match above, arguments reveal undertones of insecurity, with one partner feeling a lack of importance and the other feeling like nothing they do is ever good enough. This underlying insecurity is what fuels the negative cycle.

Before we explore the negative cycle of your relationship, let's take a closer look at relationship insecurities—the roots that feed the cycle. Here are some of the most common attachment insecurities that create fear in the relationship:

- My partner doesn't care about me and my feelings.

- My partner doesn't want to be with me anymore.

- My partner wants to be (or is) with someone else.

- My partner will continue to shut down and avoid conversations that matter to me.

- My partner will not accept me for who I am.

- My partner is falling out of love with me.

- My insecurities are pushing my partner away from me.

- My partner will abandon our relationship.

- I am not good enough for my partner.

- I am not able to count on my partner to show up for me when I need them.

- I am not worth fighting for.

- I am alone in this relationship.

- I am inadequate, and my partner can do better than me.

- Our past keeps showing up, and I can't trust my partner.

- We aren't able to have positive conversations and get over issues.

EXERCISE: What Are Your Relationship Insecurities?

Disconnection is the result of the negative cycle that, at its roots, is fertilized by attachment insecurities. So now go through the list above and put a check mark next to the ones you experience. Take a moment to really think about the deeper and more vulnerable feelings you have that lead you into your negative cycle with your partner. The problem is that you aren't feeling fully secure with them.

In your journal, explore the following:

- Which of these common relationship insecurities do you feel in your relationship, and why?

- Which of these common relationship insecurities do you think your partner feels in your relationship, and why do you think they may feel that way?

All these insecurities have a deep, underlying attachment need associated with them and need reassurance, but we tend not to tackle them directly. During conflicts, we are typically fighting for these needs to be met, but that isn't communicated in a vulnerable way that would draw our partners close. On the contrary, we tend to communicate in a way that pushes our partners farther away—the negative cycle again.

The more you know about what you're feeling deep down at your "roots," the more you will be able to catch how and why you are reacting in certain ways and make better decisions about where you want to steer the direction of your fights. And the same obviously applies to your partner. The more we can understand each other's underlying feelings, the more we can see past the B.S. and stick around to notice the deeper, rawer side of things. This creates compassion for each partner's side of the cycle.

Baggage

Now that you're aware of the insecurities that often drive conflict, let's talk about what magnifies those feelings in the first place: baggage; that is, we bring baggage with us—sometimes from our own histories, sometimes from the history of our current relationship—into our interactions with our partners.

Take the ping-pong couple above. Partner 1 is named Lian. Her mother walked out on her family when she was six years old, so she's always on high alert for signs of people leaving. Her history impacts her fears in her relationship by triggering her insecurity whenever her partner plans to spend an evening without her. Or consider Chris. His partner cheated on him the first year they were together, and now every time she goes "silent" on him, he's afraid she isn't happy with him and is connecting with someone else. He doesn't feel safe in the relationship and thus doesn't fully trust his partner.

EXERCISE: Your Typical Reactions to Insecurity

You have baggage too—virtually everyone does. It inevitably affects how you react in your relationship. Typically, when people feel hurt or scared, we try to hurt back—those thorns on our rose stems come out. What behaviors do you typically go to that are impacting your own relationship?

In your journal, write down how you often react when triggered or just circle the statements that apply below. Then go through the list a second time and then do the same for how you notice your partner reacting.

When I feel insecure in my relationship, I:

- Explain over and over how I am feeling in hopes of being heard

- Ask questions for clarification or explanation

- Feel so much overwhelming shame, I shut down

- Increase or change my tone

- Yell, scream

- Use sarcasm

- Blame, use pointing language ("You ...")

- Use global language ("always," "never," "all women," "all men")

- Threaten to end the relationship if things don't improve

- Leave the room

- Shut down, get quiet, and stop talking

- Call my partner names

- Am condescending

- Curse to express my frustration

- Have a panic attack, which ceases the conversation

- Throw things, punch things

- Push, restrain, kick, or hit my partner

- Become defensive and try to prove my side

- Criticize or nitpick at my partner

- Go into problem-solving mode and try to "fix it"

- Get intellectual and use reason and logic

- Explain to my partner why they are "wrong"

- Tell my partner what they want to hear to get them to stop (even if I don't agree with what I'm saying)

- Drink, smoke, watch porn, or use other forms of escapism

- Other: _____

EXERCISE: Your Negative Cycle

Now that you've identified your insecurities and typical behaviors, and are more aware of your partner's, it's time to look at how they contribute to the negative cycle in your relationship. This is essential, the first line of defense to break the negative cycle. We'll walk you through a few steps to help you map out your specific pattern so you can both come to a better understanding of what the other is feeling and needing. When you know what each of you is feeling and needing, you'll be able to prevent future fights. You'll stop arguing about the towels on the floor or who took the dog out last and will start addressing the actual issues and the negative cycle between you.

Naming Your Cycle:

In your journal or on a piece of paper, complete the following sentences:

1. My insecurities in the relationship are ...

2. When I have these insecurities, I often feel ...

3. These fears were created by ... [fill in with the parts of your history or relationship history that regularly impacted you]

4. The first sign from my partner that reinforces my fears is ... [fill in with your partner's behavior(s)]

5. I often first react by ... [fill in with your initial behavior(s)]

6. When I react this way, my partner must feel ...

7. My partner then reacts to me by ...

8. When my partner reacts this way, I often feel ...

9. What I am needing in these moments is ...

10. What my partner is probably needing in these moments is ...

You now have information—vital knowledge—in front of you in black and white. *This* is what defines your cycle. *This* is the problem. Not you or your partner. Rather, it's the thing that swirls between you like a tornado or the bomb always waiting to go off or an endless match of fruitless verbal ping-pong—whatever you want to call your conflict.

Granted, you are going to have a much clearer picture of your cycle if your partner has also completed this list, but even if you're figuring things out on your own, you can still do your best to represent both sides of the street here in viewing your relationship cycle—you can still figure out *a lot* from just your own awareness of what's going on.

Given all this, what would you name your cycle? One of the suggestions above, like "The Endless Ping-Pong Match" or "The Tornado"? Or can you think of something very personal and very specific to the two of you? Many of our clients have gotten quite creative with their cycle names (even using quite colorful language!). Name yours now and then write it down in your journal, along with why you chose it. Like all enemies, your cycle needs a name so you can defeat it.

TOOLS FOR YOUR TOOLBOX:
Stopping the Cycle

You and your partner are in this together. Working together against your negative cycle will help unite you and make it easier to prevent fights. Here's a step-by-step guide of what to do when you catch yourself in your negative cycle.

1. **See the pattern as the problem, not your partner as the problem.** The "oh crap, here we go" feeling means your negative cycle is creeping in. You know that feeling! Here is where you need to slow down and press the pause button. When one person jumps into a fight, the other person automatically gets pulled in. The cycle has convinced you both that you can't count on each other and that you are on separate teams. It always takes two, so to see the fighting as one person's fault will only make things worse. Instead, see that nasty cycle you just named as the problem—it sucks *both* of you in, which is why Sue Johnson calls it "the enemy." Identify the conflictual back-and-forth between you as the problem creating the wedge, *not* your partner.

2. **Acknowledge the cycle to stop the cycle.** With the pause button pressed (i.e., the blaming and defending have halted) and with your negative cycle identified as the problem, it's time to point that out. Bring the cycle into the light so you and your partner can team up against it. By calling it out when it is occurring, two positive things happen: First, you take away its power. Second, you can more quickly notice that you are on the wrong path, so you can more quickly step out of the fight. Try saying something like, "Hey, our cycle is here right now. Let's not let it win! We are working on our relationship, and we are going to figure things out." This approach removes the blaming language and fosters a team approach to fighting against the enemy (your named cycle). It takes only one person to do this for this step to be effective. Be that person.

3. **Internally reflect.** You must remember that you are part of the cycle. Now that you have called it out and avoided falling into the blame/defend madness, take time to look at what is really going on

under the surface. Begin by internally reflecting on what your body is telling you: What are some of the emotions (primary and secondary) you're noticing here? How are they showing up in your body? (Remember: noticing emotions in our bodies helps regulate our bodies and calm those emotions down.) The better you are at reading your internal signals, the easier it will be to stop these negative patterns. Identify the softer, more vulnerable emotions you're having and what type of reassurance you're really needing from your partner right now. When you express your primary emotions properly, both partners get to the root of what's going on and connect on a deeper level.

TOOLS FOR YOUR TOOLBOX:
CARES

CARES is another useful acronym to keep in mind to help stop your cycle and work toward a secure attachment with your partner:

C = Cool off: Use the calming tools provided in chapter 3 to soothe your nervous system so you have a choice in doing something different at the moment.

A = Awareness: Be aware that you are trapped in your cycle. Consciousness is key. If you don't know that you are stuck, then you won't know to look for a way out.

R = Respond, don't react: This means responding with your heart rather than falling into reaction mode (baring your thorns).

E = Engage: Don't shut down and shut off from your partner by going into hyperarousal or hypoarousal. (Recall that even when you're yelling and screaming in hyperarousal, you're still shut off from your partner, just in a very different way from withdrawing or leaving.) Instead, choose to engage with your partner from a calm and regulated place. Shutting your partner out emotionally will only fuel the fire and increase the escalation.

S = Soft: When in doubt, always go with the softest, most vulnerable feeling you are having.

Like every good plan, you've got to have a backup if things don't go as hoped. If the CARES method doesn't work when you try it with your partner, that's when you pull the emergency brake system:

> Emergency brake system: Take a half-hour negotiated break from the interaction (using the steps discussed in chapter 1). You and your partner are just too flooded now for these steps to be effective. After the break, try CARES again.

Tying It All Together

You may have noticed in this chapter that we stayed focused on our negative cycles with our partners, not on the details or specifics of our fights (such as unmade beds, unanswered texts, in-laws, or too much video gaming). In counseling, we call the topics of disagreements the "content." Focusing conversations on content is where couples get lost in the ping-pong match. Fight the urge to discuss the content of your fights and instead discuss your negative cycle.

As couples therapists, we don't help you figure out who should have unloaded the dishwasher or gotten home earlier. We concentrate on how you are talking (or not talking) about your feelings and needs around the issues. We track the cycle and help couples step out of it, so they can simmer down the intensity and do something different, something more productive, that reestablishes connection. In doing so, the content of the issues basically becomes irrelevant.

We hope your takeaway from this chapter is to avoid doing your typical moves in your cycle with your partner. Keep your side of the street clean. Avoid getting lost in the content. Instead, call out the cycle. Stop the defending/blaming game. Use chapter 2's A.R.E. tool and this chapter's CARES technique to stay connected during difficult times. And always remember why you are doing this in the first place: You are fighting for connection with your partner, for a secure attachment with your partner. You are fighting for your relationship.

CHAPTER 5

Trauma's Impact on Connection

You may feel like you are losing your mind, like your rage doesn't match the situation, or like your partner's reactions are over-the-top. You may regularly ask yourself, "Why is my partner acting so crazy?" Or worse yet, when conflict creeps in, you may automatically set your safety response in motion, such as shutting down or exiting the situation or relationship. These feelings are real, valid, and common when trauma is impacting either you or your partner.

Many times, problems in the relationships of highly escalated couples have nothing to do with the topic at hand and everything to do with trauma being unconsciously or consciously touched. Trauma is a fact of life for many high-conflict couples, and it's often very misunderstood. It is mostly associated with combat, serious or fatal accidents, sexual assault, and physical abuse; however, trauma can result from a larger variety of things.

Trauma is actually much more nuanced than often supposed, and it can arise from any number of things on life's spectrum, including not having your emotional needs met in childhood, bullying, experiencing shame at school, growing up with a parent with a mental illness, or having had a past relationship that was invalidating, controlling, or abusive. One thing about trauma, though, is certain: "Trauma almost *always* involves a violation of human connection" (Woolley 2022).

In this chapter, we hope to enlarge your understanding of how unmet needs or past attachment violations could have been traumatic for you and, if so, how that trauma is showing up in your relationship now, either triggering how you react to your partner or impacting your partner in the cycle in which the two of you are ensconced. Why is this so important? Because "[t]rauma is not just an event that took place sometime in the past; it is also the imprint left by that experience on mind, brain, and body. This imprint has ongoing consequences for how the human organism manages to survive in the present" (Van der Kolk 2015, 22).

Trauma as an Active Participant in Relationships

Trauma can interrupt our ability to respond appropriately to the issue at hand and to ask for reassurance or for our needs to be met. Events that remind our brain of the past often cause unconscious, knee-jerk responses that spiral out of control immediately, causing a waterfall of reactions inside us that, in turn, can trigger our partner's trauma. An event occurs, fear ignites, and the body goes into our fight-or-flight safety mode.

Oftentimes, couples are totally unaware of when their pasts are impacting the present moment, and this can cause a trauma-trauma reaction, in which both partners are triggering each other's past wounds without even knowing it. Clearly, these triggers perpetuate the negative cycle. As Bessel van der Kolk explains:

> When something reminds traumatized people of the past, their right brain reacts as if the traumatic event were happening in the present. But because their left brain is not working very well, they may not be aware they are reexperiencing and reenacting the past—they are just furious, terrified, enraged, ashamed, or frozen.

After the emotional storm passes, they may look for something or somebody to blame for it. They behaved the way they did because *you* were ten minutes late, or because *you* burned the potatoes (2015, 45).

Notice the inability to self-reflect and take responsibility for oneself here with the lateness and potatoes examples; instead, the blame, energy, and responsibility are projected onto someone, anyone, else. In other words, trauma interferes with people's ability to differentiate between what is happening in the present moment with their partner and what happened in the past. This can disorient their internal awareness of why they react the way they do. Their projected blame and lack of understanding seriously impact communication with others.

We've devoted an entire chapter to trauma because it's crucial to recognize the unique role it plays in high-conflict relationships. First we'll talk about the biology and impact of trauma, take a deeper look at your past traumatic experiences, and begin to observe whether these experiences influence the disconnection and escalation in your relationship. Then we'll offer some tips and tools to cope and simmer down the trauma-related escalations.

Before we dive in, let's start with some definitions so that we're all on the same page in terms of the language we'll be using in this chapter:

- By "trauma," we mean *anything* in your past that is negatively impacting your current experience in an intense way, setting off your automatic survival reactions. This can be anything from past physical abuse to being impacted by divorce to experiencing religious or racial oppression. The definition of trauma is broad.

- By "trauma response" or "dysregulation," we mean the cascading effects of experiences in your body and mind that happen in the present when experiencing exposure to a past trauma's trigger— how you feel in fight-or-flight mode (rapid heart rate, sweating palms, racing or disoriented thoughts, moodiness, rumination, anxiety, shutting down, rage, and so forth).

- By "trigger," we mean anything that can elicit a trauma response, something that consciously or subconsciously reminds you of your past trauma. It's helpful to remember that a trigger doesn't have to be exactly the same thing you experienced; it can just remind your body and mind of the trauma by resembling *some aspect of it*. Sam's trauma, for example, is triggered by flying. He experienced a lot of chaos and unpredictability in his home as a child, growing up with an alcoholic father. Now, air travel of any kind triggers him because it mirrors his past feelings of being stuck in an environment he cannot control.

- By "tender spots," we mean the sensitivities or open wounds you have to certain events in your relationships *because* of your past trauma (this can be something that has happened before, outside of, or in the relationship). Sue Johnson calls them "raw spots" and defines them as "[a] hypersensitivity formed by moments in a person's past or current relationships when an attachment need has been repeatedly neglected, ignored, or dismissed" (2008, 98–99). To give an example, for someone who was traumatized by being abandoned in their childhood, their partner shutting down, threatening to leave, or being unavailable will be a tender spot for them. (Note: Knowing your partner's tender spots is super important, so you can be aware and careful around these particular areas and not take their reactions to them personally.)

- By "regulate," we mean decreasing our triggers and getting our bodies back to baseline—out of a triggered, fight-or-flight place and back to feeling good again.

What Trauma Looks Like in a Relationship

As we mentioned in chapter 2, high-conflict couples are more likely to have trauma, which is a large factor in why their fights escalate so quickly. There are two kinds of trauma: "big T trauma" meets the criteria for posttraumatic stress disorder, and "little t trauma" has been created by an event in your past that still sends your body into a triggered, fight-or-flight response but doesn't qualify as full-on PTSD (Barhash 2017). Though the distinction between the two types of trauma is significant, interestingly, both can contribute equally to the responses you or your partner has when exposed to triggers and both can contribute equally to the escalation of conflict.

Jenni's Story

Jenni, a thirty-five-year-old married woman, grew up with two older brothers. When she was a baby, her oldest brother, Hugh, three years old at the time, despised her and was cruel to her. When they were in elementary school, her brothers would often physically fight, and she would be brought into it. As a teenager, Hugh would physically attack her, and she would access her rage to protect herself. All of this was seen by her parents as just "sibling rivalry," and all of it was normal to Jenni. Because her brothers often caused big commotions and her parents were thus regularly tending to the last disaster they'd created, Jenni grew up in the shadows, not getting her needs met. She felt unseen and invisible. She would receive praise for being the "good girl" who didn't ask for anything, so she learned that in order to maintain connection, she had to shut off her inner world and disown her internal needs and wants, calling on her rage when necessary.

Fast-forward to adulthood. Jenni has difficulty asking for what she wants, often falls into a people-pleasing role, and becomes angry when she feels slighted and unseen. In her marriage, whenever her husband looks at his phone or accidentally cuts her off when she is speaking, she instantly feels like she did when she was a kid—when nothing she did or said mattered, when she was marginalized by her own family. Within seconds, her body floods with the intensity of that familiar survival-mode reaction, and her rage immediately boils up as a coping mechanism. She begins to blame, explain, and yell.

In the grips of her trauma response, Jenni isn't able to even consider her husband's perspective and his needs. He's left feeling confused, unsure why the conversation went so far south so quickly, so he tries to explain his side of things: that he was just finishing up an article he was reading. But his attempts to repair the rift by explaining only feel more invalidating for her. Her history of trauma is getting in the way of her attuning to her partner's experience, and she doesn't understand that he is impacted by it as well. So, wham, just like that, they're in their negative cycle: She blames him, he defends, she gets louder, he backs off. The more he backs off, the more invalidated she feels. She slams doors and threatens to leave as a plea to be seen. The more volatile she gets, the farther he backs away to protect himself.

Jenni's experience doesn't fit the mold of what one might typically think of as trauma. But we can clearly observe here the emotional aftereffects of experiencing more nuanced forms of trauma and how the learned behaviors one adopts for survival end up impacting that person's adult life. Jenni's emotional scars might be invisible, but she causes herself further injury every time she shuts down on the inside in an attempt to keep the peace, or accesses her rage, like she did with her brothers. But this tactic backfires now—her behaviors have taught the people in her life that she doesn't need anything, that she's "fine" when she's actually dying on the inside, longing to be seen and feel connected. Particularly in her home, with her husband, she is unable to reach for her needs with him in a vulnerable way and instead turns to her trusty rage, which comes on fast and furious. When she does eventually tire of shutting down her emotions and attempt to find her voice, it comes out as critical, blaming, and angry toward him.

Jenni's responses and reactions are unintentional, but they are what's familiar to her. She's become quite talented at denying her needs and accessing her anger, but that isn't necessary anymore. She is safe now and no longer a child, no longer exposed to her family's dynamic. She is simply having a disagreement with her partner—something that all couples have all the time; the situation is uncomfortable, sure, but .

it's still completely safe. But Jenni's past trauma is blocking her access to that knowledge. Instead of acting from a safe place, she reacts in jolting ways that mirror the past—and are disproportionate to the current situation.

EXERCISE: Do You Have Trauma in Your Relationship?

People who have experienced trauma try to lock it up and "just move on." However, unprocessed trauma (that is, trauma that is undiscussed, unhealed, or undealt with) plays a role in our lives in the present. This is because, when it comes to trauma, the past comes alive in the present moment through the reactions in our bodies. Lisa Palmer-Olsen (2022) explains that high conflict in relationships is caused by the inability to discriminate between what's happening now, what happened in the past with the trauma, and what has happened in the relationship. Awareness of each feeling, thought, or reaction that is impacted by your history, your partner's history, and your history together is key.

Here is a list of common signs and symptoms of trauma and how it may show up in your relationship. Go through it with your partner, each of you writing down the indicators that apply to you, then share your lists. If you are going through it alone, write down in your journal what applies to you, then make a separate list, perhaps in a different-colored pen, that you think applies to your partner. As you do so, consider the ways in which these trauma symptoms are unintentionally or intentionally impacting your relationship.

- Difficulty concentrating, disassociating for a few seconds/minutes, zoning out

- Irritability, rage, quickness to anger

- Rigidity in behaviors and thoughts, inflexible boundaries

- Inability to think straight or find words to accurately express feelings

- Tendency to emotionally shut down

- Feeling numb

- Flooding thoughts of worst-case scenarios, regular scans for danger

- Intense reactions to unpredictability

- Hypervigilance, or being "on edge" during triggering situations

- Reactions that don't fit the situation, "zero to sixty" reactions

- Dreams/nightmares that replay the traumatic event

- Rumination about triggering things or the trauma itself

- Feeling unsafe when, logically, things are probably safe

- Feeling self-protective, especially around triggers

- Difficulty sleeping

- Difficulty getting close to others, pushing others away

- Mental flashes of trauma images (dissociations or flashbacks)

- Exaggerated startle responses

- Self-destructive and impulsive behavior, including threats to harm oneself

- Threats to leave the relationship

- Physical reactions to triggering stimuli (rapid heartbeat, sweaty palms, tingling hands and feet, difficulty breathing, racing thoughts)

- Avoidance of people, places, and things that might ignite uncomfortable feelings

- Social withdrawal or social isolation

- Feeling permanently damaged, inadequate, hopeless; feelings of shame, despair, or lack of motivation

- Self-loathing

- Impaired relationships with others

- Use/overuse of substances or distractions (alcohol, drugs, video games, porn) to numb the body

The Past Becomes the Present

A key defining feature of trauma, as introduced above, is that *the past becomes the present* in both the mind and the body; even if the mind knows things are different now, the body remembers. This can be incredibly disorienting in relationships, in which people are hoping to build new connections and have new experiences of love and intimacy, because when a trigger unexpectedly pops up, the person with the trauma goes into a fearful reactive mode and the other person becomes confused and hurt, not knowing what's going on. It can get to the point where it feels like you're walking through a minefield, unsure of where to step, and when a bomb inevitably does go off with no warning, the explosion is too large for the situation.

When the mind shifts to the past, the body becomes dysregulated. This reaction often results in disconnection with your partner, which typically starts the relationship's negative cycle up again. All of this makes it very difficult for partners to build intimacy and address concerns in a healthy way.

Let's look at the case of a war veteran, as we have worked with many in our practice. Loud noises or Fourth of July fireworks send them on high alert and can immediately transport them to the past. Cognitively, they know they're safe at home, no longer on the battlefield, and it was simply a pot that crashed to the floor in the kitchen. But no matter how much awareness they have, their body remembers the danger of what certain sights, sounds, and smells used to mean and reacts accordingly. Although individuals diagnosed with PTSD often experience the full battery of trauma symptoms—difficulty sleeping and relaxing, routinely being on high alert, having racing thoughts, an exaggerated startle response—in more predictable cases of trauma such as combat experience, partners are often (but not always) aware of their mate's past experiences and the difficulties they're facing. Armed with this knowledge and an actual label they can confront (PTSD), they will hopefully seek out help to process the trauma and deal with it together.

Unfortunately, other forms of trauma—"little t trauma"—aren't as evident. Here, the metaphorical land mines aren't as easy to spot and track and their cause is often unclear to the couple. It's disorienting for both partners when one of those explosions unexpectedly goes off, leaving both utterly confused as to what just happened.

Tyler's Story

Tyler's trauma is like that. His parents had a highly tumultuous marriage, with big, loud blowups that resulted in long periods of silence afterward. Not just silence—either his mother or his father was known to just disappear for days at a time following one of their huge rows, and Tyler never knew when they were coming back … or if they were coming back. This went on for years. His childhood experience was very unpredictable, very stressful, and quite precarious. Although he does not meet all of the criteria for a PTSD diagnosis, he is experiencing trauma symptoms that are impacting his relationship now in a significant way. When he met and married Destiny, he vowed that their union would be nothing like his parents', and he felt sure he could make this happen by choosing a woman as steady, stable, calm, and reliable as Destiny.

But guess what? Tyler and Destiny don't have the perfectly peaceful and tranquil marriage he dreamed of. Though they love each other deeply, they often find themselves at odds about the same things over and over, and neither seems to understand what's going on. A typical encounter looks like this: Destiny has a difficult job as an ER nurse and prefers to decompress after work. So sometimes she'll tell Tyler she's too tired to go out to eat like he proposed or she'll sneak off to the bedroom to read for a little alone downtime. Any such action like this is interpreted in Tyler's body, if not his mind, as an act of disappearance, rejection, even betrayal. His fight-or-flight response kicks in—his body's way of protecting itself from a dangerous situation that feels all too familiar—and before he can even think a rational thought, he's following Destiny around, raising his voice at her, accusing her of not caring about him, and asking her why he's even there if she's just going to ignore him. He's looking for any kind of response from her (any kind of response is better than no response, remember?), which is preferable to the deafening silence he witnessed so often between his parents.

In response to Tyler bursting open the bedroom door and yelling at her, Destiny just stares at him like, Are you crazy? What's wrong with you? I'm just reading! She's having serious doubts about her husband right now, thinking he's just too needy and controlling. She's flabbergasted, at a loss—just looks down at her book, turns her body sideways away from him. This only seems to enrage Tyler more. Eventually, she can't help herself—she takes the bait and starts yelling back, trying to defend her position and get Tyler to see how out of control he's acting, how unfair. Then—bam!—here they are again, right in the middle of their negative cycle, having another escalated fight that sounds just like the fight they had last week, and neither even knows how they got there that fast. Again.

In this dynamic, Tyler's alarm system is set to go off much quicker and more easily than in someone without past trauma. And because Destiny is unaware of how his past has impacted him, unaware that he's slipped from the present moment into a past experience, she feels like she doesn't even know who this screaming man before her is— nothing like the thoughtful and quiet beau who courted her. But Tyler's underlying attachment insecurities and fight-or-flight response are driving his outbursts, and he doesn't know how to get back to that regulated space in which he can talk to his wife rationally and reasonably and share his deeper primary emotions. Instead, all he feels is his anger, and all Destiny sees is his anger.

Does any of this sound familiar? The past-becomes-the-present response that we've been discussing is an extremely common result of any kind of trauma and is a key factor leading to high conflict. We all have tender spots that we've accumulated over our lives, and when one of those spots is poked, anyone and everyone is vulnerable to subconsciously connecting a present occurrence to a past hurt and then physically and emotionally responding to the injury.

This is very adaptive—it's the body's and brain's way of protecting you from a threat you've experienced before. But you no longer need this protection. You're not in the past, with a mean teacher or a critical grandparent or bullies at school or an emotionally absent parent at home. Like Jenni and Tyler, you are in the here and now with a partner who loves you and wants to understand you, if only they had the knowledge to do so: awareness of your tender spots (and you of theirs) and the real primary emotions underneath the secondary emotions that are driving their confrontational behaviors.

Dr. Palmer-Olsen (2022) likens the trauma response in couples to a bear and squirrel analogy. The "bear" is the trauma experience from some point in your past. When you initially encountered the bear, it was scary, dangerous, and unhealthy for you, so it's only reasonable that it has left you on alert, constantly on the lookout for the bear's reappearance so you can defend yourself if and when that happens. This puts you on edge, distrustful, in a general state of unease at the mere thought of the bear reappearing.

But then a squirrel enters the scene. Your body and your mind don't actually see a squirrel, though. It's a fluffy, brown animal that has come upon you unawares, so your brain says, *Yup, probably the same thing!* and sends you into reactionary mode, with all those cascading trauma responses discussed before. Then, even after your mind logically realizes that you are safe now—*Whew! Luckily, that's just a squirrel! No big deal!*—the body lags behind, still controlled by your stress hormones. You don't just automatically return to equilibrium, but instead stay in the heightened state of hyperarousal (maybe even doubting your own reality: *Am I sure that was just a squirrel?*) as your body continues to remember and react to the past trauma.

This can be extremely frustrating for trauma survivors because they're now aware the situation is safe, but they've been hijacked by their bodies, swept away in the fight-or-flight trauma response that feels out of their control. It's equally unsettling for their partners, who find their mates' responses to a harmless squirrel quite disorienting. Say your partner's phone dings (the squirrel) indicating a text message. Is it really just Aunt Millie … or is it actually "the other woman" from years ago (the bear)? Too late—the trigger has gone off and with it comes an intense fight-or-flight response in the body and in the mind. In essence, "The bear keeps running the show" (Palmer-Olsen 2022).

> **TIP** One of the keys to solving the trap of high conflict is helping the couple tell the difference (either cognitively or within their body) between the bear of the past that is impacting their relationship and the harmless squirrel of the present moment. Once they can differentiate between the two, they can learn to regulate the body and relearn the feeling of safety. When the squirrel does show up, they can then stay physically connected to themselves and to their partner.

Finding Comfort in the Chaos

The biology of trauma sets us up for failure in our relationships when we get triggered. When we get triggered, the speech centers in our brain go inactive. Because of this, it is difficult for us to realize what is going on and put thoughts and feelings into words (Van der Kolk 2015). At times, we are just reacting to the triggers from a place of trauma rather than responding to our partners with intentionality and thoughtfulness. What's more, when our bodies are in a reactionary fight-or-flight mode, we go offline and are unable to show up with A.R.E.—accessibility, responsiveness, and engagement—to connect with our partners.

You may have asked yourself why you always seem attracted to the "bad boy" or "bad girl" or those with lots of baggage. It is common for people who have experienced trauma to lean toward chaos, toward the difficult relationships filled with conflict, volatility, and unpredictability, because it's what their body knows. It's familiar to them. There is a sort of comfort of the familiar that draws those who have experienced trauma toward chaos, as they can become comfortable with the distress and often feel bored without it. Thus chaotic and unpredictable relationships can be experienced as "exciting," akin to seeking out thrilling experiences and events. The desire to feel the stress hormones can actually make the body feel balanced and *normal*.

What does this mean for you? The disorganized and unpredictable behaviors from your partner (or from yourself) may lead you to believe that they enjoy starting fights and like all the drama around them, but they are actually struggling with balancing their nervous system. The reaction is just familiar and what the body knows, so it's drawn to it. On the other hand, when there's a shutdown—mute-during-conflict behaviors from your partner (or from yourself)—it might feel like there is a lack of caring here, but what is really happening is that the brain can't verbalize what emotions are occurring. The left frontal lobe of the cortex goes offline, and then the shutdown happens. Trauma impacts the mind, body, and nervous system in significant ways that end up impacting relationships.

EXERCISE: Identifying Your Tender Spots

Understanding why your body responds the way it does is a prerequisite for dealing with trauma in a high-conflict relationship. Let's start the way we have before, with you just pressing your own pause button, acknowledging your behavior, and figuring out where it is coming from.

More specifically, take a moment right now to rewind the tape of your life. Is there an event or theme you have experienced throughout your life that you think is contributing to the trauma symptoms you identified in yourself in the last exercise? If so, consider how it is showing up in your life now. Get out your journal and explore the reactions you notice from yourself (and your partner), along with their origins. You do not need to relive the past or share unwanted details; just explore in general terms *what* the reaction is about and *where* you think it comes from.

Example: *I notice myself getting hot, anxious, overwhelmed, and wanting to escape when my partner starts yelling at me. I think it's because it reminds me of when my dad used to yell at me after I didn't do well at a sports game. I always felt not good enough and like a failure in those moments. It makes me feel like a failure all over again.*

If you feel emotionally safe doing so, share the insights you wrote with your partner using the steps in the next exercise. Feel free to own your confidentiality and have agency over how much or how little you choose to share. But it's important to remember that having your partner know your tender spots and having you know theirs is a fantastic way to mindfully care for each other around these sensitive areas. Think of these tender spots like potholes in the road: when you know you're there, you can gently maneuver around them, which is both respectful of past hurts and creates safety while driving the vehicle of your relationship.

EXERCISE: How to Share Tender Spots in Three Steps

Before we can even broach the process of how to safely share sensitive information with your partner, it needs to be clarified that this will be a very different experience if you are the only one doing the sharing versus both of you doing the sharing.

If you're both reading this book and walking through the steps together, then proceed as follows. But if you're the only one doing the work here, your partner will simply not have the same level of understanding or the same skill set you're developing to navigate these conversations in a soft and validating matter, let alone start them.

So the choice is entirely yours. If it doesn't feel emotionally safe for you to have deeply emotional conversations with your partner aimed at bettering your relationship—if you've tried but it only blows up in your face, making the cycle worse or being used against you—then hold off on this exercise for now, or perhaps consider bringing in a qualified third party to help facilitate such conversations for you. But recall that it takes only one of you to step outside the cycle to change it. So if you decide to proceed with the exercise, start off by explicitly letting your partner know what you need from them in the conversation—if you don't tell them, they can't know, and you'd be setting both of you up for failure.

Now that you've identified your tender spots, here's a three-step process you can follow to increase your chances of having a successful exchange in which you and your partner actually hear each other (note: this process applies to any topic, not just sharing tender spots):

1. **Set a date.** Find a time to have the conversation when both of you will be emotionally tuned in; this means free from distractions and in a good headspace. (For example, don't do it right before bed, with children present, or while substances are being used.) It's best to plan this in advance.

2. **Follow a speaker-listener format.** This means agreeing to have only one speaker at a time; the other actively listens when their partner is speaking. Successful active listening looks like turning your body toward your partner, making eye contact, and using non-verbal communication that shows you're in the conversation, like nodding along with an open expression on your face.

3. **Validate each other.** This step is extremely important, as it's critical for each partner to feel heard. To accomplish this, each and every time before switching roles, the listener (a) repeats back what they've heard, paraphrasing the speaker's message, and then (b) states why it indeed makes sense. (Remember that validation does not have to mean that you *agree* with what your partner is saying; it just means that you're hearing their reality and can *understand* why it makes sense to them.) Validating language doesn't have to be perfect or fancy—a lot of people worry about this, but you don't need to sound like a therapist here. You're just trying to show your partner that they're not alone, they're not crazy, and their experience is valid. Example: *"It sounds like you shut down when you hear me get loud because it reminds you of how your dad was when you were into sports. That makes sense that it would feel triggering for you; that sucks."*

EXERCISE: Identifying Your Trauma in Your Negative Cycle

Trauma integrates itself into your negative cycle with your partner in a significant way. Your body's response creates a reaction on your end (typically, you'll either pursue your partner or withdraw from your partner as a result of your trauma trigger), and your partner will react to your reaction. What your partner does or says in response often exacerbates the situation—making you feel even more triggered, so the dysregulated emotions and behaviors continue—and around and around it goes.

Sometimes our own trauma can trigger our partner's trauma, leading to a trauma-trauma-triggered reaction cycle. In this cycle, both partners end up dysregulated and unable to connect.

In your journal, consider how trauma impacts your negative cycle by exploring the following:

My tender spot is _____ .

When I am triggered, I tend to _____ [insert behavior(s)].

When my partner sees this, they tend to _____ [insert behavior(s)].

Underneath my behavior, I am feeling _____ [insert primary emotion].

What I am needing emotionally from my partner is _____ [insert emotional need].

What I am needing from myself is _____ [insert healthy coping skill].

Now go back through the same questions and look at them from your partner's perspective. Do you have an idea of what your partner may be experiencing?

Here's an example from Tyler earlier in the chapter:

My tender spot is seeing my partner distancing from me.

When I am triggered, I tend to rage and make threats to be seen.

When my partner sees this, she tends to back away even more.

Underneath my behavior, I am feeling so scared that she will leave me.

What I am needing emotionally from my partner is connection with her and to feel loved and safe.

What I am needing from myself is to take a thirty-minute break, to create space to emotionally regulate. I can take some deep breaths, do a grounding exercise, and remind myself that I am safe now.

Trying New Things Leads to Change

By now, you know what trauma looks like in a relationship and how it can impact the dynamics of the relationship in a destructive way—how it insinuates itself into the established negative cycle in which all kinds of attachment needs and insecurities are also swirling around. To halt this old cycle before it can really get rolling, you have to try new approaches. Applying your newfound understanding of each other's triggers and treading carefully around newly identified tender spots is one such approach. You're working toward a corrective experience to replace the tired, unsuccessful patterns that keep you stuck in automatic trauma responses and self-protective, defensive stances. You're working to shift from being stuck in the past to being fully present in the moment.

When you and your partner react differently to each other during a triggering event, your bodies can learn to react differently. This is based on research on neuroplasticity, which shows that human behavior can only change through the vehicle of new experiences (Lamagna 2022). So the next time one of those land mines goes off, you don't have to react to it as you always have; rather, your job—each of your jobs—is to press the pause button, acknowledge the explosion, and respond in a new way that is safe for both of you. What you're doing is allowing this new experience to change your neurobiology.

When you practice this over and over and your neurobiology begins to change, it's the new positive responses that become the new habit to stop the negative cycle in its tracks and simmer down the brewing confrontation. As Scott Woolley words it, "The antidote to trauma is safe human connection" (2022). Reacting to your partner's trauma responses by providing this safe, human connection has an immense influence on helping them heal from the trauma with corrective emotional experiences. You and your partner really do have the power to change things for the better!

TOOLS FOR YOUR TOOLBOX:
Helping Each Other Through Tender Spots

When you or your partner notices feeling triggered, you can help each other! This is possible now because you have shared your tender spots with each other, because you're aware of them now; as such, this awareness can serve as your anchor to the present moment and help you there. Your attachment to your partner can become your "golden ticket" to regulating your trauma. We call this *co-regulation*: using another safe, healthy, and secure person to help us calm down and come back into the present moment, away from our triggers.

Here's how you can support each other when tender spots get triggered:

- **Call it out.** When you notice that one of your tender spots has been touched, put it into words for your partner right away. Just this insight will decrease the likelihood that you'll slide into your reactionary behaviors and fall into your negative cycle. You have a context for what is going on now; you can ask for help. You can say, "Hey, I just noticed that my body's feeling triggered right now" or "My tender spot just got stepped on. Let's take a pause for a minute."

- **Invite your partner to call it out.** This can be risky because we don't always like it when someone else points out something about us that we have a hard time accepting. But we've found it to be extremely helpful when partners are open to naming the tender spot for their mate when they see it impacting the interaction. You just need to do so in a soft, noncritical, and nonblaming way, like "Hey, hon, I know you're upset right now about me being late for the PTA meeting, but maybe something more is going on? I think this may have triggered one of your tender spots about feeling unimportant. Want to talk it out?"

⊙ **Take a break.** When triggered, one or both of you may need time to regulate before jumping into a conversation about it. Just because you're now aware of your trauma responses doesn't mean they're going to go away. That's why you need to set aside time for yourself to apply your coping skills to help your body come back to baseline. Then, from a place of emotional regulation—and with your new tool of co-regulation with each other—productive improvements can be made.

How to Regulate on Your Own

The best and quickest way to regulate on your own, to return yourself to the here and now, is to make your body realize that it's safe enough to calm down. You can do this in a number of ways, but just trying to reason your way out of it isn't going to work. That's because trauma lives in the body, so we need to tackle trauma triggers at a body level.

Psychiatry professor Stephen Porges helps us understand this through his work on "polyvagal theory" (PsychAlive 2018), which involves the vagus nerve, a part of the parasympathetic nervous system that helps us relax, calm down, feel safe, and recover from trauma triggers. The term "vagal tone" refers to how strong your vagus nerve is, or how good it is at relaxing your body. When we are triggered into a trauma response, activating this nerve helps the body calm down and turn that response off. It also helps in reactivating the prefrontal cortex—the part of your brain that deals with logic (PsychAlive 2018; Abramson 2020; Recovery Direct n.d.).

Here are some ways to train and tone your vagus nerve:

- Use cold water (drink it, put an ice pack on your face, take a cold shower, go outside in cold weather).

- Use mindful, deep breathing (just three deep breaths is sufficient), with your exhale double the length (in seconds) of your inhale.

- Make a social connection (even just texting a friend if you don't have time for a call).

- Make eye contact with another person.

- Pull your body back to the present with mindful awareness (look around your space, notice what is around you, describe the objects you see).

- Acknowledge the tension in your body and take steps to relax it.

- Observe your thoughts without judgment.

- Engage your five senses (go outside, garden, exercise, cook, dance to music you love).

- Lie on your back with your legs perpendicular to your body against a wall.

You can also change your thoughts to change your perception of the experience, for example:

- *This is just an argument. No one is dying. We will get back to a good place.* (This can help you stop exit planning.)

- *He is just having a hard time talking. He isn't abandoning me. He still loves me.* (This can help stop abandonment triggers.)

- *She is just mad. I don't need to fix it. This is just an emotion. I can keep myself safe.* (This will remind you that emotions are safe and you have agency and control over how you choose to respond.)

Quick Tips: How to Regulate Midcycle

In reading the above section, you may have been thinking, *There's no way I'm going to stop in the middle of a heated episode and plunge myself in cold water! How ridiculous!* Okay, we hear you. So here are some pointers to set yourself up for success:

1. Start soft, slow, and kind.

2. Use the "Call It Out" step from the previous toolbox section as soon as you notice feeling triggered.

3. Pick a coping skill or two from earlier in the book to try out.

4. Explicitly tell your partner which skill you are going to use and why.

5. Give it a set period of time.

6. Tell your partner that you are going to engage in this skill for the set period of time in order to help your connection and so that you come back together more effectively. (This will help reduce abandonment triggers, which are common here.)

7. Come back together at the agreed-upon time.

Example: "*Hey, babe, I am feeling triggered right now. I am going to take a shower to cool off. Can we reconnect when I'm done in twenty minutes? I want to do this so that we can have a positive conversation. I want to stay connected to you.*"

EXERCISE: What Helps You Regulate?

This exercise is like a fire drill for the next time you experience a trigger to practice what you can do to turn down your fight, flight, freeze, or appease response and turn up your vagal tone. You'll want to start with a mild trigger first. Just like you'd never want your first football practice to be playing at the

Super Bowl, you don't want to start with a deep issue—more like something you find slightly annoying to one of your tender spots, like yet another spam call interrupting your personal time or yet another instance of your partner's damp gym clothes on the floor.

The next time you encounter this type of mild trigger, *right* when you feel yourself starting to experience it (in that zero-to-sixty impulsive reactionary period), rate your stress level on a scale of 0 to 10 (where 0 = not at all distressed and 10 = hugely distressed). Jot this number down in your journal.

Next, pick any of the steps and any number of the steps listed earlier to activate your vagus nerve and engage in them ideally for twenty minutes (although we get that sometimes isn't possible).

Lastly, rate your mood again now, after you've employed one of the regulation strategies. Did your number go down?

This can look like this:

Trigger: *Friend not texting me back*

Distress level: *5*

Coping tool: *Drank cold water while taking deep breaths for seven minutes*

Distress level after: *3*

Try out all of the strategies at one time or another and record in your journal which ones work best for you, which are the least helpful, and what your "safety plan" will be for the next time you experience a trigger.

How to Let Your Partner Help You Regulate

So we've talked about navigating tender spots, halting your negative cycle before it becomes full-blown, and self-regulation during triggering episodes, but what if you're having a difficult time regulating yourself? What can you do then? You can ask for your partner's assistance, that's what!

Recall that co-regulation means having another person to help us move through potentially escalating situations and return to baseline. Let your partner be that person for you when you're triggered, asking them to remind you to try something different than what you usually do when you're in this space. As explained earlier, the best way to move out of old patterns is to experience something new, so practice the tenets of neurobiology with your partner.

Co-regulation can look like anything you want or need in that moment: seeking comfort with a hug, holding hands to feel connected, practicing deep breathing together, any of the steps to improve your vagal tone listed in this chapter, or address hypo- or hyperarousal (covered in chapter 3).

With your new awareness of your tender spots, let your partner know you're being triggered and ask for what you need from them in a soft, open way. Your partner can't hug a cactus, so fight the urge to be prickly toward them when you're going through a difficult experience. Give them the opportunity to provide you with a new experience and be there for you in a different way.

What to Do When Your Partner Is Triggered

On the flip side, your partner will also have tender spots that get provoked in the relationship. When you realize you've accidentally (or, let's be honest, sometimes intentionally) stepped on one of them, here are some measures to take to keep you both emotionally regulated.

Try to anticipate the triggers. Sometimes when we're driving down a street, we can see the potholes up ahead in time to avoid them. Other times, you'll just hit one without warning. But once you're aware of your partner's trigger points, you can predict when they might occur and prepare for them—for example, drinking alcohol, anniversary dates, situations involving unpredictability, and certain sights, sounds, or smells. Your awareness of these upcoming triggers puts you in a better position to be ready for them. You can talk to your partner about them and devise a plan together on how to protect the relationship from them.

Breathe. Your partner's behaviors can be extremely frustrating, such as blaming and questioning. Don't react to them, just breathe first. Rewiring how your body and your partner's body respond to triggers is a slow process, and breathing through it will help you get there. Be patient when your partner is triggered; they're not choosing to be impacted, they simply *are* impacted. A person with trauma may need to talk about the event over and over again, and even though this may feel like no movement on your end, it can be extremely helpful for your partner to talk through things with you. It's part of the healing process; it's progress. Avoid the temptation to defend or attack back when you're criticized. Just take a breath and focus on preventing yourself from being pulled into the negative cycle.

It's not you, it's them. Don't take the reactions to triggers personally. If your loved one seems distant, irritable, or closed off, this might not have anything to do with you or your relationship and everything to do with their own trauma. You can help them with the trauma, but you didn't create the trauma.

Don't pressure your partner into talking. Don't try to force your loved one to open up when they don't want to. Let them know you're there if and when they want to talk. You can even ask them what you can do to help. But give them the space they need to process what they're going through. You are not responsible for them, but you *can* be a support for them when they need it.

Tying It All Together

When it comes to healing trauma, it's important to engage in new, safe, positive experiences that will create new neural pathways that allow for long-term change. You and your partner might trigger each other's trauma, but you can also be the way out of it for each other. It all comes back to the paramount importance of attachment in our relationships and the therapeutic nature of human connection.

This chapter required a lot of self-reflection and self-accountability. By doing this work, you are not only giving yourself the chance to heal, but you are also learning what's needed to support each other through past hurts and create a new closeness between you so you can show up for each other in a new way.

Now that you have a richer understanding of trauma and how to better deal with it, what can the two of you do to actually resolve past hurts between you? Stay with us. Stay vulnerable.

CHAPTER 6

Resolving Past Hurts

Is there a topic or theme that keeps showing up over and over again when you fight with your significant other? By this point in the book, you now know how to de-escalate conflict and halt the negative pattern, and you understand how your past (outside of this relationship) influences the present in your relationship. However, there may still be unresolved issues from your shared past together that keep getting rehashed, showing up and leaking out all over the place, causing conflict and disconnection.

These issues point to the unmet attachment needs in your relationship—the things you've been longing for but haven't received in years. Or, a significant event took place in your relationship at which point everything changed, the trust was betrayed, or the security was broken in what's known as an "attachment injury." This chapter is all about past and present unmet needs and attachment injuries—just between the two of you in your one-on-one relationship—and what to do to fix them.

Unmet Attachment Needs in Your Current Relationship

The last chapter talked about tender spots: sensitive areas that are triggering for us and that developed from unacknowledged attachment needs from past trauma. Well, tender spots can originate in our current relationships too, particularly when we have needs that have been going unmet for a long, long time, which is the focus of our discussion here. We all have attachment needs in our relationships, and if these needs are repeatedly neglected or abandoned by our partners, it's a pretty safe prediction that this is going to cause a wound that will eventually need to be properly healed.

Here are some examples of common unmet attachment needs in couples:

- The *need to feel desired by a partner*, as a couple navigates a nonexistent, or very difficult, sexual relationship

- The *need to feel seen and heard*, as a couple navigates the impact of years of a partner shutting down, defending, and/or withdrawing

- The *need to feel unconditionally accepted and good enough*, as a couple navigates the impact of years of a partner's criticism and nagging

- The *need to feel safe and secure*, as a couple navigates the impact of threats to leave the relationship when difficulties arise

EXERCISE: Identifying Unmet Needs

Which of the unmet attachment needs listed above apply to you? Can you think of more or other unmet needs specific to your relationship? Write them down in your journal. Then start to explore the impact each unmet attachment need has on the negative cycle in your relationship with the following prompts:

When my needs of _____ aren't being met, I tend to react
by _____.

When my partner's needs of _____ aren't being met, they
tend to react by _____.

When our needs aren't met, it causes us to _____.

If possible, go over these prompts together, with only one "speaker" and
one "listener" at a time, having each partner acknowledge and validate what
the other said. Then switch. Go slowly and try to stick to simple language to
complete the prompts. Take about five minutes to share.

The Importance of Vulnerability

Remember when we talked about flying trapeze communication in chapter
2? How both people must properly play their role with just the right timing
for the partnership to work? This is the same for couples reaching for their
needs to be met. For the exchange to be emotionally safe, the flyer has to
communicate clearly that a jump is coming so the catcher can be aware
and ready for the jump. If a partner simply asks for what they need without
the element of vulnerability added in, it will come out as criticism every
time, and the reach will be unsuccessful. Read that again: *If you ask for
what you need without vulnerability, it will come out as criticism every time.*
People tend to tell their partner what they need, but they have no clue it is
coming out critical—and it pushes their partner away.

Saying "I need you to listen to me" is like a trapeze artist jumping
without communication, reaching in a way that puts the catcher in danger
of dropping them. That is because the need is not being communicated in
a vulnerable and safe way that will set them both up for success. The
catcher won't "take the catch" and the flyer will fall into the net, so setting
the catcher up for success is just as important in completing the trick as
taking the jump in the first place.

At the same time, even if the flyer informs the catcher properly and starts the trick by being vulnerable, if the catcher doesn't show up to catch them, the partner will still fall. As the flyer, even if you do everything "right," there's still a chance you may not be caught. And yet you have to try nevertheless—you can't succeed unless you try.

As the flyer, you simply have to take the risk and trust the process, being vulnerable by communicating your primary emotions as well as your needs; in turn, you have to show up for your partner when they reach for you too. This can sound like, "I feel terrified and hurt when I hear you threatening to end our relationship. I need to feel safe with you right now." A clear, honest, and vulnerable "jump" like that equates to the perfect timing for both swings; it sets you up for the reach, your partner for the catch, and both of you for a safe and successful interaction. Vulnerability is the key—it's what creates the perfect timing.

Here's the equation for successful communication:

$$\text{Vulnerability} + \text{Need} = \text{Connection}$$

EXERCISE: Practicing Flying Trapeze Communication

Invite your partner to revisit a recent disagreement you had to try out this form of communication. First, determine who will be the flyer (the speaker) and who will be the catcher (the listener). (We recommend that whichever partner is typically the withdrawer between the two of you be the speaker first.) It might seem scary to take this leap, but it's worth it, because the payoff is increased trust in each other and showing up for each other. Here are the steps:

1. **Flyer:** Similar to the trapeze artist indicating they are ready with "Listo!" you need to inform your partner that you are about to jump: "I am about to take a risk because you matter to me." This allows your partner to know that this is vulnerable and scary for you and that you need them to catch you.

2. **Catcher:** In the world of trapeze, it's time for the catcher's "Hep!" which means you're here for the flyer. Show your partner that you are ready by setting down your phone, turning off the television, and turning your body toward your partner. Tell them explicitly that you are ready and that you are in the conversation.

3. **Flyer:** Share your primary emotions (not the content, not your secondary emotions) about the specific event that happened. Dig deep into the vulnerability. Allow yourself to feel your emotions and let your partner see them. Focus on using "I" statements here, rather than "you" statements.

4. **Catcher:** Give signs you are there for your partner, holding out for the catch and listening to them. Say "uh-huh" and nod your head, and validate your partner's emotions. (Reminder: You don't have to agree to validate; what matters here is that your partner can tell you're hearing what they're communicating and that their experience is important to you.)

5. **Flyer:** Ask for what you need *right now* for comfort.

6. **Catcher:** Provide that comfort.

How did that go? Journal about this new experience you just tried with your partner.

The Necessity of Healing from Attachment Injuries

"That event changed everything between us." "I can never trust her again." "I feel broken now." These phrases are common when there has been an unresolved betrayal or attachment injury in a relationship. An attachment injury is a sense of betrayal and/or abandonment within your bond with your partner that occurs during a critical moment when you needed them and they weren't there for you (Johnson 2008). Attachment injuries and betrayals can consist of more than just affairs (although that's a big one);

they also include significant life moments of stress or vulnerability in which one partner did not show up, either intentionally or unintentionally, leaving their partner all alone (Johnson, Makinen, and Millikin 2001).

In therapy, couples often complain that, over the years, their communication issues and fighting have gotten worse. Once we dig in, we commonly find at the origin of these issues an emotional wound that has never healed properly. They tried to "get over it" and "move on," but the wound unintentionally created a layer of uncertainty in their connection.

Unresolved betrayals and attachment injuries are often at the root of high-conflict relationships. They create a general lack of safety, causing a partner to regularly be in protective mode, on alert for the danger to happen again. Think of lime juice: If it is squirted on a scar, it is painless. However, if you still have an open wound, the lime juice stings *badly*. Like the lime juice, an unresolved attachment injury from the past causes serious pain in the present, no matter how long ago the injury occurred. (Note that this is also like the trauma we discussed in the previous chapter, because, let's face it, an episode of betrayal or abandonment in a relationship *is* traumatic.)

The relationship was once safe and you felt like you could count on your partner, but then one day everything changed. The security was broken, and so the way you think of and view your partner changed as well. This understandably impacts the offending partner too, who may be left without a road map for how to repair the damage and make things better when nothing seems to be working.

In these moments of distress, when the hurt partner is unable to reach their mate (physically or emotionally) for their needs to be met, an emotional wound is created. The unmet need then sends a message to the hurt partner about their mate: *I can't count on you when I need you the most. I must take care of myself because you won't be there for me.* We know that counting on others for care and support is an essential attachment need, so when it's not met, there are repercussions. The hurt partner understandably puts their walls up and starts throwing out bombs as a way to protect themselves. But in so doing, the relationship turns into a battlefield instead of a united team playing on the same field, and the offending partner begins responding to the attacks. The result is a high-conflict couple.

Here are some common attachment injuries:

Lack of support when:

- Baby is born

- Experiencing a miscarriage

- Going through the death of a loved one

- Having a traumatic experience

- Experiencing health issues

Secrets and betrayals when having:

- Affairs (sexual, emotional, virtual)

- Financial problems

- Addictions

If you are reeling from an attachment injury, no matter how long ago it happened, you're both going through a lot right now. Your heart may be aching (or protected by a massive wall and grenades), and various feelings are moving through you both. We know it's difficult, but we also want to assure you that, having worked with *hundreds* of couples going through attachment injuries, these ruptures are fixable. They *can* be repaired. You can do this—you and your partner just have to put in the work.

The process of healing and recovering from these wounds is key to decreasing conflict, because if issues are left unresolved, they fester below the surface and stay there, often worsening over time. Yet the research shows that attachment injuries don't heal effectively until the couple's negative cycle has cooled off (Johnson and Makinen 2006). This is good news for you because it means that all the hard work you have done up to this point—such as learning how to calm things down, knowing what your negative pattern is, and owning the past issues that show up in yourself—is going to greatly help you reach your goal of decreased conflict in your relationship. By getting this far, you have set yourself up for success and created the proper foundation for attachment injuries to properly heal.

In our ongoing analogy of building your "dream home," this equates to making the necessary repairs to all the internal stuff lurking behind the walls, like the plumbing and the electrical wiring. If it's faulty, it'll keep acting up at inopportune moments. Here is where we go in and help you fix it all, so the house is safe and sound moving forward.

Why "Just Move On" Doesn't Work

This topic is worth its own discussion because we hear it so often. Couples come in to see us all the time because they want, so desperately, to "just move on." We hear things like, "Our relationship would be better if we could just move forward," "I don't want to dwell on the past anymore," or "He just needs to get over it." Or here's one of our favorites: "We just need a vacation, then we'll feel better." Um, no. Wrong.

Emotional wounds are similar to physical cuts. A large scrape or gash must be tended to properly if it's to heal correctly; otherwise, it continues to bleed, it oozes pus, it can get infected, and if the infection isn't treated with antibiotics, the injury can even begin to impair other parts of the body. An attachment injury is no different—if not attended to, it will get worse and infect other parts of your relationship.

So you or your partner can't just "move on." The fighting will only get worse until the source of it is properly dealt with. Acknowledging this is important for both of you in the relationship, because neither partner can simply repair things, or "get over it," on their own. This is *not* a one-person job! No, this will require both of you, which is why it is of course best to move through the rest of this chapter together. But if that's not going to happen, you will still glean insights about how these injuries have impacted your cycle and learn tools for how to repair them when the time comes. As you proceed, just remember that the time frame is irrelevant here: some attachment injuries occurred as recently as yesterday, and others happened decades ago. Either way, working together to repair the wound properly is what will enable you to move forward.

The Impact of Attachment Injuries

When there is a rupture in the relationship bond, trust is broken. The injured partner begins to see the offending partner differently—their experience of them, and of the relationship, begins to shift in a significant way. A person they once felt safe with suddenly became unsafe. This shift can leak into other areas, causing a protective stance, disconnection, and high conflict. The injured partner can feel as if the entire relationship was a lie.

In response, the injurer can begin to feel hopeless, like nothing they can do will help. They can feel stuck, frustrated with their partner for "not moving forward," and disappointed in themselves for not knowing how to help. Often overlooked, offending partners may also feel extreme amounts of shame—not only for the events that happened in the first place, but also for the resulting impact on the relationship.

Any type of injury can cause trauma or a trauma-like response (the "little t trauma" we discussed earlier). Affairs and other types of wounds are very traumatic and can cause trauma symptoms, especially if the relationship was feeling safe and is no longer safe.

There are multiple impacts from betrayals:

- Long conversations that happen over and over (and never stop)

- Extreme, "zero to sixty" reactions

- More fighting, yelling, screaming

- Increased sexual engagement that has you feeling more connected (common right after betrayals are revealed)

- Deeper conversations that feel like they are bringing you closer (again, common right after betrayals are revealed)

- Roller coaster of emotions

- Small and insignificant issues that become big fights fast

- Fear of losing the relationship and family and/or threats to end the relationship

- Living in the unknown

- Ambivalence (unsure if staying or leaving)

- Reexperiencing symptoms (such as dreams or flashbacks about the attachment injury)

- Analysis of the past to try to make sense of what happened

- Irritability, feeling on edge

- Self-blame for partner's behavior

- Shame and embarrassment

- Attempts to understand why it happened by asking questions nonstop

- Hypervigilance and constant scanning of the relationship for safety

- Monitoring the other partner by checking their phone, social media, or whereabouts

Cassandra and Trini's Story

How a significant attachment injury plays out in a couple can be seen with Cassandra and Trini, who began couples therapy to work on "communication issues" and to improve intimacy. During the first few sessions, their negative cycle was identified and explored—namely, Cassandra critically attacking and Trini defending and distancing in response. It all began four years ago, when Trini, a member of the military, was deployed toward the end of Cassandra's pregnancy.

Though the deployment was neither Trini's choice nor her "fault," it nevertheless resulted in an attachment injury for Cassandra because Trini was not available during a significant time of need for Cassandra—a time made all the more difficult by Cassandra experiencing birth complications. Although she logically knew that Trini had no control of not being home for the birth of their daughter, she felt all alone and scared and experienced Trini's absence as abandonment.

Her view of Trini being "her person," the special someone she could always rely on, shifted. Cassandra now feels she can't fully depend on her wife. She attacks. She can't give in and trust her one hundred percent anymore. For her part, Trini is extremely frustrated with Cassandra. She takes pride in serving her country and sees Cassandra's resentment of her duty as Cassandra not respecting her sacrifice. She can't understand how Cassandra can't understand that the timing of the deployment was not her choice.

It was tremendously hard for Trini, as well, to not have been there for her daughter's birth. Her unspoken guilt over this causes her to shut down, go quiet, and pull away. Although the couple used to fight about this, the issue never got resolved, and even though the broken trust between them doesn't directly come up anymore, it created something new: their negative cycle of attack/distance.

They're not as connected as they once were, and they are much quicker to anger. The more they fight, the more it reinforces a lack of safety for both. Because their wound was never properly treated, it's left a bleeding gash in their relationship that will require attachment injury repair work in counseling to heal.

Another Layer of Emotional Wounds: The Impact of Secretive Attachment Injuries

Trini and Cassandra's attachment injury—the unfortunate timing of Trini's deployment—was out in the open from the start, with both partners aware of it at the same time; they just didn't know it would cause such a rupture in their bond. But attachment injuries that have a hidden element to them add another level of complication to relationship dynamics. In betrayals that are secretive, such as emotional, sexual, or virtual affairs, *how* the partner finds out about the betrayal is critical for determining the depth of the wound and the level of its injury on the relationship. If your relationship has been inflicted by a secret attachment injury, read this section carefully, because this type of injury carries its own long-term impacts.

First, consider the injured partner's gut feelings and safety. Did the injured partner have alarms going off, telling them that something wasn't right, but the injurer assured them it was safe...*when it wasn't?* If so, the wound is going to be very deep, and the ability to rebuild trust will take a lot of focus and work. This is because the injured partner was falsely reassured by the injurer; they believed them, chose to trust them over their own gut and intuition, so they feel doubly betrayed: by themselves and by their lying partner. This is a form of gaslighting, and it's very damaging because it makes the injured partner question their own reality.

Second, consider how the secret became exposed. Did the injurer confess on their own? This is the best-case scenario; although still painful, it at least establishes a context in which trust can be rebuilt. But if the injured partner stumbled upon the truth themselves—if a friend shared it with them, if they discovered it by researching and digging for information, or if they accidentally saw something they then couldn't unsee—this will cause a deeper wound. Their partner never confided in them and now they'll never know whether they ever would have. This is an unarguable breach of trust, and it causes the one betrayed to become hypervigilant, always on the lookout for signs that dishonesty is happening again, lurking around every corner. This is not paranoia or mere suspicion; infidelity happened in the past, so it could very well happen again.

Lastly, was the information revealed honestly all at once? Or did it dribble out over time, not only elongating full disclosure of the story but elongating the injured partner's pain? The impact of the dribble effect can be severely detrimental to a relationship, as the injured partner's safety and security are drastically lacking. They'll never truly know whether they got the full story of what happened from their partner, so how can they ever truly know that they're getting the full story about anything now?

A secret betrayal coming to the fore is like a meteor crashing to the earth: it's going to be bad no matter what; but *how* it hits will determine the extent of the damage. If you are currently causing an attachment injury or betrayal, you need to aim for the least amount of damage possible. You can't avoid the impact, but you can reduce the size and speed of the meteor by intentionally controlling how you disclose the information to your partner.

Here are our recommendations for disclosure of secrets that have the best possible outcomes in a bad situation:

1. Be the one to tell your partner about the secret to ensure the information comes from *you* rather than from other sources; this will somewhat lessen the negative effects on the relationship.

2. If your partner has had suspicions, gut feelings, or alarms going off, validate them. Don't make them doubt their own truth because of your dishonesty.

3. Fully disclose *all information* (no matter how scary this may be) regarding the secret all at once to avoid the dribble effect over time. If not, the new information that slowly leaks out drip by drip will continue to destroy the trust and make things even worse.

4. Own your part of why and how the event happened. Take full responsibility.

5. Your behaviors and words need to match from here on out. Your words have lost their value and you can no longer provide your partner with reassurance in this way, so your behaviors must send the same message to help your words regain value.

Successful Repair and Recovery

Couples need four elements to successfully recover from attachment injury trauma (Johnson, Makinen, and Millikin 2001):

1. First, they need to have a shared story of what happened with the event. (Does the couple agree on what the injury even is? It is important to get on the same page about what's being discussed. This is sometimes more difficult than imagined.)

2. Then they need to understand and make sense of the impact this event has had on each other.

3. Next, they need to fully process and move through the emotions the event caused that are impacting their cycle now. (This will require vulnerability and A.R.E.—accessibility, responsiveness, and engagement—with each other.)

4. Ultimately, they need to have a new "corrective" experience around healing—to create a new experience together that wasn't available at the time of the injury.

The goal of the following sections is to walk you through these four elements with your partner in order to reach successful recovery from any attachment injuries that are still impacting your relationship.

Neuroplasticity and the Corrective Emotional Experience

Human beings recover from injuries through new, positive, and corrective experiences (Lamagna 2022). Deep and lasting change doesn't come about just by thinking about something differently or gaining insight about it—we need to actually do something different that is felt on a new level. Have you ever vowed that you'd respond differently to your partner next time you have a fight only to be unable to follow through on your resolve during the heated conversation? It's hard to just change. Add to that the complication of a still-open and bleeding wound, and it can be impossible.

But having a new positive interaction, or what we call a "corrective emotional experience," is an elemental part of EFT because it works to repair wounds. The power of actual felt emotional experiences sets the stage to allow change to happen. We are highly emotional beings—our emotions help us organize and make sense of our inner and outer realities, and they've been shown to be integral to the process of change for couples in therapy (Obegi and Berant 2009).

Corrective experiences help us develop new responses in ourselves and with our partners. This is because new experiences create new neural connections and new pathways in our brains. *This* is how change happens both inside of ourselves and within our relationships (Lamagna 2022). The brain is an amazing and resilient muscle that is highly adaptable—it's neuroplasticity in action when we add something new to our environment or interactions and watch the brain adapt to it. So let's get to work using neuroplasticity to your advantage to create corrective emotional experiences with your partner.

Identifying the Shared Story

The first step in creating the change we're seeking here is to pinpoint the wound and the defining moment when the trust was broken. This is necessary so that the betrayed partner has a clear understanding of why the injury happened as they start to make sense of their partner's distressing actions. It's also imperative to have an understanding of exactly what took place for accurate integration of and recovery from the trauma (Johnson, Makinen, and Millikin 2001).

Identifying the Impact on the Injured Partner and Relationship

An attachment injury makes an impact on how we view our partner. Most often, it sends the message that we can no longer count on them, that it's unsafe to expose our heart to them, and that we now have to walk through life on our own. Those are some pretty big impacts!

Feeling unsafe with your own partner puts you in protection mode—in one of the fight-or-flight responses—which does not allow you to access your primary emotions and resolve things tenderly and softly with your partner. Instead, you interrogate, pry, blame, attack. For a partner who's been cheated on, for example, the mere ring of their mate's phone can instantly bare the wound.

In this next exercise, you are going to make some sense of these deep emotions and understand how they show up in your negative cycle.

EXERCISE: Writing Out the Impact on the Injured Partner and Relationship

If your partner is open to it, invite them to participate in this exercise with you. You'll again be using your journal to explore some probing questions. Review your answers together, one at a time, taking turns as dedicated speaker and listener, validating each other as you go and working toward mutual understanding.

As you've done before, proceed slowly and softly, trying to be precise and succinct in your answers to the prompts below. Reflect on *your* part of the pattern, take responsibility for your behaviors, and allow your partner to reflect on theirs. Any cycle is a circle, so both of you play a part in going round and round, both of you impact each other. It's never a "one person started it and the other is just reacting" dynamic. The injury may be the trigger that sets off the cycle, but you *both* keep it going, regardless of the initial emotional wound.

I get triggered by _____ *[fill in with the event that recalls the injury]*. When I am triggered, I feel _____ *[fill in with primary emotion(s)]*. I then react by _____ *[behavior]*. When I react this way, my goal is _____. Unfortunately, you probably get the message that _____ and then feel _____ *[your partner's primary emotion(s)]*. When you feel this way, you react by _____ *[behavior]*. This sends me the message that _____ and then I feel _____ *[primary emotion]*, and the cycle repeats itself all over again.

Now put the behaviors of your negative cycle together:

The more I _____ *[behavior]*, the more you _____ *[behavior]*, and then the more I _____ *[behavior]*.

Example from Cassandra and Trini:

Cassandra: *I get triggered when I think about you being deployed when Brooke was born. When I am triggered, I feel scared and sad all over again. I then react by nitpicking at you and criticizing you. And sometimes yelling. When I react this way, my goal is for you to see me, see my pain, and see my hurt. Unfortunately, you probably get the message that you aren't good enough and aren't getting it right and feel sad and scared. When you feel this way, you react by pulling away from me and distancing yourself. This sends me the message that my feelings don't matter and I end up feeling alone and afraid all over again, and the cycle repeats itself all over again.*

And here's the example of their cycle put together:

The more I yell and criticize, the more you pull away and shut down, and then the more I yell and criticize.

Processing the Emotions

The cycle is what causes disconnection. When we haven't fully processed and repaired the deeper experience, we stay stuck in our cycles, so we aren't talking about what is *really* going on underneath the cycle. After the root cause of distress has been made clear and the impact it has had on the injured partner and on the relationship is understood, it's time for the hurt partner to have a chance to discuss the *depth* of the impact the event has had on them. This is a necessary step in fully processing the deeper emotions in order to repair the experience.

Opportunity for Repair

Apologizing is a great way to work toward repair. However, *how* an apology is delivered makes it or breaks it. Bad apologies are characterized by just wanting to quickly pacify the situation and not holding the partner's experience. They are defensive in nature, they don't take ownership, and they don't adequately access empathy and remorse.

Examples of bad apologies:

- "I'M SORRY!" (in a pleading, angry, or impatient tone).

- "I'm sorry, *okay?* I've told you a thousand times I am sorry!" (dismissive, minimizing, lack of responsibility taking).

- "I've said I am sorry. What else do you want from me?" (dismissive, minimizing, lack of responsibility taking).

- "I'm sorry, but …" (the "but" negates the apology).

- "I'm sorry that this happened" (lack of responsibility taking).

- "I'm sorry" (in a robotic tone that indicates no understanding of the pain, with a blank stare and no heart attached; emotionless; saying it just to say it).

- "I'm sorry you feel that way" (blaming, lack of responsibility taking).

- "I'm sorry. Can we just have fun now?" (dismissive, minimizing).

Good apologies, in contrast, go beyond the words spoken to also express a real understanding of *why* there is remorse and an ability to sit with the discomfort of that. When making the apology, your heart must be connected to your words in a way that both you and your partner can feel—the genuineness should be palpable. This can be hard to do, but it's super important because a heartfelt apology sends the message: "I see you, I hear you, and I understand." Thus it integrates so much of what we've been talking about, incorporating multiple elements of the steps toward recovery from relationship trauma through being A.R.E. with your partner.

To make an apology even more meaningful, employ nonverbal cues as appropriate: putting your phone down, body language that shows you're open and present, turning toward your partner, reaching for their hand, being patient during moments of tears, allowing yourself to reveal your own emotions while your partner is speaking, and remaining available to them.

Examples of good apologies:

- "I'm so sorry I wasn't there for you when you really needed me. It makes sense to me why you would feel hurt, scared, and sad about that. It really impacts me to know about the pain I have caused you. I am here for you now." (Shows a clear understanding of the impact of the pain and the ability to sit in the emotions of the experience.)

- "I am so sorry that I have been unavailable to you for the last few years. I feel terrible knowing the pain that I have caused you. I understand how painful that must have been for you to take care of the kids and the house and be so lonely while I was working so much. It makes sense why you have been feeling unseen and unheard in our relationship and that your needs have gone unmet. I want to know how this has felt for you. I want to be here for you now." (Shows genuine interest in the pain, does not try to make it "go away," doesn't rush through the message, allows integration of the shared emotions.)

EXERCISE: A New Kind of Experience for a New Outcome

Sue Johnson and Judy Makinen (2006) developed the Attachment Injury Resolution Model, or AIRM, for therapists to help couples repair injuries. Couples who take a deep dive into the depth of their emotional experiences using this model find success in healing. Taking AIRM as our inspiration, we modified the model to fit how we use it in our therapy sessions. It takes the four elements needed for attachment injury recovery and condenses them into an easy-to-use speaker-listener exercise.

Research shows that for this model to be most effective, it is crucial to hear, experience deeply, and engage with the primary emotions that have been revealed in a new way that provides a new experience (Lamagna 2022; Johnson and Makinen 2006). So you don't want or need to be so concerned about the actual specifics of the injurious event. Rather, move out of your head and into your heart. Prioritize the rupture and the repair. This is what will allow you to resolve the injury and truly be able to "move on."

And there's no better time to start than now! So, taking everything you learned about attachment injuries above, let's go through this process, which breaks down the approach to a newly created corrective experience by acknowledging the hurt, attending to the unmet needs, and aiming to repair the wound.

The "fix" requires both of you for it to work. You have to show up for each other, listen to each other, validate each other, and comfort each other in ways you likely haven't in the past. The injured partner will have to take the risk of breaking down the barriers and putting their heart back into the relationship, while the offending partner will need to push through the discomfort and the urge to disappear or withdraw, holding their partner's heart safe, letting them know that their pain matters to them, and being there for them now in a way they weren't able to be back then.

If you are going through this book solo, consider this a great opportunity to deepen your learning about how to have this kind of conversation in your relationship if and when repair feels possible. Share as much of this process with your partner as you're comfortable with, in hopes of gaining their buy-in for when they're ready to work on the repair with you.

Step 1:

- **Sharing the Hurt.** Start with the injured partner as the speaker, the one who will share the wound or the unmet attachment need here. Take the risk of sharing your experience from a vulnerable, soft place. Focus on the pain, emphasizing the hurt, without attaching criticism, blame, or anger; instead, address the rawer feelings of hurt, sadness, and fear. This is where the primary emotions are shared, steering clear of the secondary emotions. It's critical to access the emotional pain and not feel emotionally muted or held back while sharing.

- **Seeing the Hurt.** Simultaneously, while the speaker is speaking, the listener's job is to tune in to, validate, and see the pain—with tenderness, not defensiveness. *Acknowledge that the hurt partner's feelings make sense and are understandable.* Give responses that indicate you are listening with body language (eye contact, holding your partner's hand, nodding) and with short, affirming utterances, like "Uh-huh," "I get it," "That makes sense," and "Tell me more." Take the time to attend to your partner and don't try to rush them through their pain as a shortcut to fixing it.

Step 2:

- **Diving in Deeper.** Here, the speaker goes deeper, continuing to share what lies at the core of the hurt. The speaker should prioritize the emotional vulnerability here, specifically as it relates to the grief and fears surrounding the losses that occurred. This may be grief around the loss of safety and security in the relationship and/or the fear of losing your partner altogether.

- **Catching and Apologizing.** Again, simultaneously, while the speaker is speaking, the listener's role is to catch their partner (as in the trapeze analogy) by responding with tenderness. They jumped—so now you catch them gently and in a safe and caring manner. Take ownership of your actions and summarize what you've just heard your partner say to make sure everything is being understood. Apologize nondefensively, expressing deep concern and genuine remorse. (Refer back to the examples of good apologies above if needed.)

Step 3:

- **Making the Ask.** Now the speaker clearly asks for what they need in this moment, what their partner can provide them in the here and now. Perhaps reassurance is needed or a hug or an acknowledgment that their partner truly understands the depth of their pain. This allows the partner to show up *now* in a way that wasn't an option before.

- **Showing Up.** Once the speaker makes clear what they need, the listener shows up by providing whatever type of comfort was requested. Then check in with your partner to make sure you got it right and see whether they need anything more from you right now. This ability to show up in the moment the way you didn't back at the time of the attachment injury can prove an antidote to the traumatic experience.

Next, after you feel ready, switch roles. The listener becomes the speaker and has an equal opportunity to share their pain and needs.

Tying It All Together

Congratulations on making it through such a difficult but worthwhile leg of the journey—that took strength and bravery. The pain you've experienced from the attachment injuries in your relationship and the unmet needs surrounding those hurts has been very real and valid. It's entirely normal to feel exhausted by them.

And this is all leading you toward your goal of decreased conflict in your relationship. Only once you've identified and resolved your attachment injuries can you finally move forward as a couple. Upon successful completion of these steps, the structural components of your "dream home" are now in place and you're poised to start the fun part. You're well on your way to the third and final stage of the EFT framework—the integration/consolidation stage, in which you'll be moving into, decorating, nesting in, and making this new house your permanent residence. But first, a pit stop into an integral and indispensable topic for all couples: sex.

CHAPTER 7

Let's Talk About Sex

Sex is such a multifaceted topic. In the life of a romantic couple, it can be exciting, arousing, bonding, and fun, yet it can also be triggering, distancing, and disappointing when it contributes to the negative cycle of a couple, often without them even knowing it.

We hear it all in our sessions: "I'm too tired." "I had a headache." "He's not interested." "She's not interested." "It's never enough." "Our sex life is nothing like what you see in the movies." Because we're meeting with couples experiencing problems, it's not surprising that they're often sexually dissatisfied, living as roommates, and not getting their needs met—all of which causes further disconnection and conflict. It's not uncommon for individuals to cut off physical intimacy when feeling heightened levels of distress. Without emotional security, sexual vulnerability does not feel safe.

In this chapter, we're going to review the role of sex as a form of connection, explain the different types of sexual dynamics, and address how your negative relationship cycle has been impacting your sex life. We'll also talk about how that secure emotional attachment you've been working toward carries over into a happier, healthier sexual attachment with your partner. Luckily for all of us, recent research findings have shown that EFT is effective in strengthening sexual satisfaction and bonding in couples who use it (Johnson, Simakhodskaya, and Moran 2018).

A Few Basics to Start

Arousal is a back-and-forth dance between partners. One partner's excitement spills over into the other partner's and vice versa, which of course enhances the experience for both. Additionally, the bonding hormone, oxytocin, gets released during sex, furthering our deep connection to our partners in a healthy, safe, and positive way. But there are different levels and types of desire.

Some individuals have *spontaneous* desire—they're easily aroused, always ready to go, think about sex frequently, and often use it to relieve stress. These people can be "turned on" within seconds.

Those with *responsive* desire, however, don't just flick a switch to the "on" position. Rather, their life stressors and negative stimuli need to be turned "off" before they can get in the right headspace for sex. Their hypervigilance needs to be turned down, they need to be feeling connected in the relationship, and their environment contributes a great deal to their sexual arousal.

All of this is to say that sex is truly a personal, reciprocal, co-created process, wherein the outcome of what the couple creates together is greater than the sum of its parts. It's a fundamental and essential part of your love relationship; given its importance, it makes sense that in high-conflict couples, the sexual arena is yet another element that can cause conflict and is impacted by conflict when partners aren't in sync.

Diversify Your Need Fulfillment

As important as sex is in a relationship (and as fulfilling as it can be), we want to acknowledge that attachment needs—such as feeling connected, valued, wanted, and desired—should be met in various ways. They shouldn't just be met on the physical side of the relationship spectrum, where sex is the only way a couple connects; and they shouldn't just be met on the verbal side of the spectrum, where communication is the only way a couple connects. It's best to use the whole spectrum to find opportunities to connect with your partner everywhere and in all ways. Similar to diversifying your funds in an investment portfolio, you want to diversify the sources through which you and your partner are getting your attachment needs met.

It's common for one partner to need emotional closeness to be sexual and the other partner to need a sexual connection to open up emotionally. In reality, we need flexibility between the two—a combination of multiple aspects of connectivity to diversify our connection resources. In his book *The Five Love Languages*, author Gary Chapman (1995) identifies the ways in which individuals prefer to get their needs met, including quality time, words of affirmation, physical touch, receiving gifts, and acts of service. This is not an exhaustive list of how people meet or receive attachment needs, but it's a way to look at the language between couples in a simple, straightforward way.

How else can you stock your "portfolio" of need fulfillment with your partner? Maybe you enjoy sharing hilarious memes with each other—connecting through humor and fun. Maybe you have special nicknames for each other that are private and sacred to just you two. Maybe you feel valued by your partner when they respect boundaries with your family members and demonstrate their trustworthiness. All of these forms of intimacy on the relationship spectrum—and many more—build toward that secure attachment with your partner, toward your "dream home." It takes more than just talk or just touch. It takes all the wild and wonderful things in between to meet each other's attachment needs.

Safety First

Sex is actually an attachment need—we all need to feel desired and wanted by our partners. We want the security of knowing we have an effect on our partner in an intimate way and that they want to get close to us—*really* close to us. We keep driving home the importance of connectivity and attachment needs, and this applies equally to sex as it does to the entirety of your relationship.

To get where we want to be sexually, we must first build a solid base, focusing on the safety and security between the two of you overall. In therapy, we have a saying: "Safe is sexy." The safer each partner feels in the relationship, the sexier things will be between them. Recent research shows that in relationships, our attachment needs of safety and security, when combined with our sexuality, leads to a fulfilling sexual relationship (Johnson, Simakhodskaya, and Moran 2018).

We are wired to put safety first—to feel safe first—and *then* we can explore true closeness and maximum intimacy. We're not talking about "safety" in terms of the way someone will "turn off" themselves emotionally to "get off" during one-night stands or casual sexual encounters. Here, we're talking about safety in terms of our basic comfort with the closeness and vulnerability in a relationship and how that affects our expression and experience of sex in the relationship. We're talking about emotional safety.

If one partner is uncomfortable with the closeness and vulnerability in their relationship, either because of their own past or because of the lack of security in the relationship (or both), they may slowly retreat from physical touch and withdraw from sexual connection to protect themselves. But living without affection, touch, and sex is a short-term tactic to deal with a long-term problem: the real problem is that there is a lack of security and safety in the relationship, a lack of secure attachment.

TOOLS FOR YOUR TOOLBOX:
Talk, Talk, Talk

Let's be honest: Sex is an extremely vulnerable act. Although things tend to be hypersexualized or portrayed in a cavalier way in our culture, the reality is that sex is a very vulnerable thing to do with another person, especially when you add in the goal of connecting deeply with your partner through sex. This is why you and your partner *need* to feel seen, heard, and understood when talking about changing sexual dynamics. What's going to help you work toward that safety? A combination of talking, checking in with each other, and slowing things down.

Talk, talk, talk. We can't emphasize this enough. Many people need to work on saying "yes" more often to their partner's pursuit of physical intimacy, while many others need to focus on enhancing the relationship connection so they'll hear "yes" more often. Either way, both require conversations. An Elvis Presley song asks for "a little less conversation, a little more action;" we're asking for the opposite: a *lot* more conversation before diving into the action.

Action is critical, yes, but to enhance your sex life, we recommend talking about sex when you're not having sex as a means to strengthen the intimate safety that comes with secure attachment. Talk about your fantasies, needs, feelings, insecurities, and vulnerabilities. Be curious about why you aren't having sex *and* talk about what happens when you are having sex. Even during sex, check in with each other on how it is feeling and how it is going. This doesn't need to be excessive or anxious (the anxious sex dynamic is one we'll discuss a little later in this chapter), but make sure you are attuned enough with your partner to know how they are doing and feeling and what they're needing in the moment. And share the same on your end.

For the spontaneous sexual desire types, think of these conversations as foreplay. Research has shown again and again that couples who talk about sex regularly have more sex and have better sex than those who don't. Of those who can't talk about sex with each other comfortably, only 9 percent of them say they are satisfied sexually (Gottman 2011). If that's not reason enough to want to talk about sex with your partner, consider how much open communication builds up that secure attachment that creates an optimal sex life. And be A.R.E. here—slow down your pace enough to be accessible, responsive, and engaged with your partner. If you aren't, you may miss their cues.

For the responsive sexual desire types, talking about sex means becoming more flexible, asking for what you want and need so you can feel safe enough to respond sexually, and being aware of the vulnerability it takes for your partner to ask for sexual connection. This may look like asking your partner to sit and talk together for half an hour or so before diving in or reminding your partner that connecting sexually is important to you, too, even though you have needs that need to be met first. It's also helping your partner understand that you need to turn off the mental noise in order to turn on the sexual desire.

So talk, talk, talk to create a win, win, win!

Understanding Your Sexual Dynamic

Arousal and communication are certainly not the only components to consider in the sexual relationship of a couple. Here we will go over the many different types of sexual dynamics that show up in relationships. The first step in moving toward a mutually fulfilling sex life with your partner is identifying which, if any, problematic sexual dynamics are at work in your relationship, contributing to your negative cycle. Only once you are aware of them can you know what to do about them. Note that more than one of these sexual dynamics may apply—that's common and normal! There is overlap within these dynamics. We will then give you tools on how to deal with each one in your relationship.

Unavailable Sex Dynamic

In this dynamic, the couple doesn't feel safe or connected. One of them is not emotionally available. And yet they're so hungry for connection that one of them (or sometimes both of them) reaches for sex as the only way of feeling loved, cared for, and desired. But as we mentioned above, a couple shouldn't rely on sex as the sole source of feeding attachment needs and security in the relationship.

Amanda and Miguel have been married for fifteen years. Miguel has struggled with the trauma that resulted from being raised by a single mother who was addicted to drugs. Quite early in his life, he had to learn to shut off his emotions just to make it through. Once he was grown and out of his mother's apartment, he locked up all of his trauma in a vaulted room…but you can't just pick and choose what to leave out of an internal vault; unfortunately, Miguel locked away all of his other emotions too.

His adaptive and protective coping mechanisms have helped him carry on, but Amanda experiences him as checked out, uncaring, and inaccessible to her in virtually all areas of the relationship, including the bedroom. Although he shows sexual interest in her, she doesn't feel he's really *there* when they're in bed any more than when they're not. But from Miguel's perspective, he wants to connect with his wife; he doesn't know how to do that emotionally, so he reaches for her physically.

In response, though, Amanda isn't getting her attachment needs met in the relationship due to Miguel's emotional unavailability, so she starts to withdraw from him sexually in a relationship that doesn't feel safe to her. Eventually, she just avoids his advances.

Makeup Sex Dynamic

Fighting happens, and then the makeup sex is on point. It's nice to feel that reconnection with your partner, but you don't want to depend on it as your only way of having an intimate bond or a sense of resolution and repair. This can become a bad habit for couples, whereby they may even subconsciously (or consciously) get in hellish fights just to get to the makeup sex! What they're really doing is avoiding the root of the emotional conflict, and when you do that, you can never get to long-term resolution of the problem. As a result, resentment can begin to build.

This dynamic can become especially dangerous to the security in a relationship because a pattern gets ingrained that intimacy and conflict go hand and hand, that in order to have sexual closeness, we must go through combat. It can also create a dangerous pattern in which one partner doesn't really want makeup sex but feels compelled to go through with it to stop the fighting.

White-Knuckling It Dynamic

This is when you want connection, but your body is triggered by your past experiences and yet you push yourself through sex—ignoring the triggers, the pain, the trauma. You think you're going through the proper bodily motions, but your partner can actually pick up on your discomfort and misinterpret it as a sign that you don't want them. This dynamic can even present as an automatic response; for example, one partner's hand might push their partner's hand away without even knowing it.

During the night, Julie's stepdad would sexually molest her when she was an adolescent. Now, even though her husband is safe, respectful, and emotionally engaged with her, her body tightens when he pursues her sexually. She goes into freeze response and disassociates while they have sex. Logically, she *knows* her husband is safe, but her body reacts as if he is unsafe. She white-knuckles her way through their sexual encounters because she wants closeness and connection with her husband, but she doesn't share her pain with him. And even though her husband can tell something is off, he doesn't ask her what's wrong, too afraid of the rejection he might hear. He simply thinks she doesn't desire him.

Freezing Dynamic

The freeze dynamic happens when one or both partners stop reaching for sex (or never have reached). When someone doesn't reach for sex, their partner naturally assumes it's due to a lack of interest in them, a loss of desire for them, which leads to disconnection.

Olivia lived for years without getting touched. Growing up, her mother was way too emotionally dangerous. Everything was always about her mom's emotions, her anxious push-pull attachment style. Her mother would either push to get love or threaten to leave to get love, so Olivia experienced an "I hate you, don't leave me" vibe from her. In response, Olivia created her own emotional safety by removing closeness to her mother—closeness to anyone, really, including anyone's touch. This was actually an incredibly smart coping mechanism for a kid, but she ended up building an invisible fortress around herself. This felt necessary in order to protect herself and survive.

Fast-forward to when she started dating her partner, Kenji, who is a very affectionate person. When he'd lean in for a kiss, Olivia knew it was "normal" to kiss him back, but it never felt natural to her; inside, she'd stiffen up. When snuggles on the couch would happen, she would instinctually push him away without realizing it. When they would have sex, rarely, Kenji would initiate, and she would freeze up and be on edge, but she never took the leap of having a vulnerable conversation with Kenji in which she took ownership of what was going on in her body and honestly communicated what she needed.

So Kenji has been left in the dark. He originally thought she was just sexually timid and that he could "fix" things by regularly talking about sex, encouraging more sex, and pushing for different types of sex. But after a while, he had no other choice but to start attaching his own meaning to her unresponsiveness, thinking: *She doesn't want me.* Now they're caught in a cycle that neither one of them truly understands.

Anxious/Shame-Based Dynamic

Have you ever had racing thoughts before, during, or after sex, such as *I'm not good enough* or *Did they think that was okay?* or *I wonder how I compare to their ex?* What about fears about failure to climax, insecurity about what your body looks like, or worries about your sexual performance? These negative thoughts and concerns can cause a cascading effect of anxiety to ripple through the body. And this anxiety can shut down sexual interactions on both an emotional and a physical level.

Anxiety, as a secondary emotion, is a sex inhibitor, blocking off the core emotion of sexual excitement as the body focuses on protecting itself rather than relaxing into the experience. This is actually a common dynamic for men who struggle with erections (the fear of not performing takes over) and for LGBTQIA+ couples as well. When partners experienced institutional, cultural, family, peer, or any other type of discrimination and shaming messages around their sexuality, they may have internalized these messages after long and painful exposure to them. This then materializes in negative thoughts, like *Am I doing something wrong?* or *I am dirty* or *Is there something wrong with me?*

Peter was a pastor's son, raised in a home where his entire life revolved around religion: avoiding sin, living minute by minute in the specific ways expected of him, and neglecting the normal aspects of childhood. He had to live according to the rigid rules of his household to gain his family's approval, with helicopter parents who allowed him no privacy and respected no boundaries. Thus, sexual fear and shame became his constant companions.

Now, in his relationship with his girlfriend, his anxiety makes it difficult to maintain an erection. Fearful of not being able to meet *her* expectations, he pulls away from her, causing her to feel confused, rejected, and undesirable. As the physical distance between them grows, so does their negative cycle of shame and hurt.

"Just Sex" Dynamic

We all just want a quickie sometimes—going right to the main event—but when this becomes the norm in a relationship, it signals an avoidance of lovemaking, the kind of sex that's emotionally vulnerable. When it's exclusively about the physical sensations, often fast-paced and intense, there's no heart (and sometimes no strings) attached.

People who subscribe to the "just sex" dynamic get freaked out by the vulnerability of sex, so it's safer to just engage without any real connection. It doesn't mean they don't love or want their mate, but they have a difficult time experiencing or asking for closeness. So the sex is then emotionally empty, leaving the partner feeling devoid of intimacy, just used for the quick thrill. It's actually a protective device for the person using this dynamic, but that's not understood on the receiving end.

The end result is two emotionally unfulfilled lovers not getting their attachment needs met and, thus, disconnection impacting their negative cycle.

Don't Talk About It Dynamic

You may want it, you may be upset about it, but you won't ever talk about it! In the "don't talk about it" dynamic, both partners stay quiet—it's like sexual shyness on steroids. This dynamic is characterized by one or both partners being fearful of discussing sex, fearful of sharing their sexual fantasies, needs, or desires, and fearful of hearing their partner's sexual fantasies, needs, or desires. There can also be the fear of not being good enough. But when the conversations never happen, the problem can never be resolved.

Pursue/Withdraw Dynamic

In this dynamic, one partner pushes for sex and the other pulls way. In fact, the more one partner pushes, the more the other pulls away. The pursuing partner may have a higher sexual drive than the other, and when their usual advances are rebuffed, they'll begin chasing sex through other routes, like dropping regular hints, making sexual jokes, using passive-aggressive language, blaming, or criticizing. This comes from a place of internalizing the lack of sex, taking it personally, perhaps not feeling good enough or desired, as well as feeling sexually frustrated. But the more frustrated the pursuer becomes in not achieving the sexual connection they crave, the more disconnected the other partner feels—backing away, just dodging the commentary, and ignoring the jokes. It's a perpetual cycle that leads nowhere.

Betrayal Dynamic

This dynamic develops when one or both partners have violated the relationship with sexual addiction, multiple affairs, and/or compulsive or secretive porn use in the past. The betrayal around sexual safety has been ongoing and chronic. Sometimes this results in a partner having sex when they really don't want to—they just do it as a plea for connection. They are fearful of losing their partner to the violations again, so they use sex as a way to prevent future betrayals or other sexual violations from happening. It's as if they're saying "yes" when they really mean "no." This causes a lack of sexual safety in the relationship.

Lisa Palmer-Olsen (2022) explains, "It is the most dangerous dynamic. It becomes a trauma in itself. You are being sexual with someone unsafe, and it is repetitive." This dynamic is a coping skill for both parties, she continues: "One of the partners doesn't feel the power in the relationship, does it anyway, and it forces the brain into a disassociated and disconnected place because no place feels safe. It is the only way they get a feeling of connection, so they do it anyway."

We're not talking here about sexual violence, rape, or forced sex—this all falls into the "abuse" category that we mentioned in the introduction as requiring resolution before any other relationship work can commence. But there's danger here nevertheless. Remember: safe is sexy, and when couples are trapped in the betrayal dynamic, there's a lack of safety in the relationship impeding their secure attachment.

Secure Attachment/Connected Sexual Dynamic

This is the one we're all working toward! Connected sex entails emotional attunement and responsiveness. Secure attachment in the bedroom is about being able to hold on to your own experience, track your partner's experience and respond to it, and be aware of how your interactions impact the experience together.

We've addressed the importance of flexibility in healthy relationships, and flexibility is also vital to a healthy sex dynamic. No, we're not talking about your ability to bend into a pretzel, but we are talking about being able to have fun, explore, try new things, role-play, have spontaneous sex, and express yourself without holding back. To start saying "yes" to sex more often and to not feel guilty about saying "no" when you don't feel like it.

In a healthy, connected sex dynamic, partners talk about their fears, desires, and fantasies. They're open to trying new things together and feel equally free to decline things that don't feel comfortable without fear of recrimination. Securely attached couples feel safe enough to be vulnerable with each other, sharing what's going on physically and emotionally when things feel right and not right. They can change directions when needed, they can accept and reject invitations for sex, they can stop in the middle of sex when a conversation or compromise is needed, and they can *still* stay connected through it all.

Safety and flexibility in the sexual dynamic allows for bringing in sex toys and sex fantasies without either partner being threatened by them. Having both partners check in with each other throughout the process provides a sense of reassurance to each other. There is no need for rigid rules or unspoken expectations. Couples can talk or not talk during sex. They can look in each other's eyes or close their eyes. They can have a long, drawn-out lovemaking session or a quickie in the car. The flexibility and the ongoing connection create a secure attachment.

EXERCISE: Exploring Your Sexual Dynamic

In your journal, respond to the following questions to identify your sexual dynamic and sexual cycle:

- What type of sexual dynamic does your relationship fall into? It might be a mixture of a few different dynamics, and that is totally okay.

- In what way would you like your sexual dynamic in the relationship to change?

- In what way is your negative sexual dynamic the same as your negative communication cycle, and how does that impact your relationship cycle? Conversely, how does your relationship cycle affect your sexual dynamic? In what ways do these aspects of your relationship differ?

It's Always Okay to Say No!

Before continuing on with our discussion of all the various sexual dynamics in relationships, it's important to emphasize one essential point: no matter what your sexual cycle, sexual proclivities, or sexual habits, it should *always* be okay to say no—that should *always* be an option on the table for either partner and it should *always* be respected by each partner.

In the secure attachment sexual dynamic, it's just a given, it doesn't have to be qualified. Turning down sex when you're not in the mood is simply a safe step and an acceptable part of the conversation about sex. One partner doesn't worry that their entire connection hinges on saying "yes" to sex all the time, and the other partner doesn't worry that hearing a "no" means they're not desired or good enough for their partner. Instead, their intimacy needs in the relationship are diversified enough so that these needs are getting met from multiple places.

But regardless of the current sexual dynamic that characterizes your relationship on this path we've been traveling toward a healthy, connected sexual dynamic, make a rule for yourself right now: *do not force your body to have sex if you do not want to.* If you do, the brain will begin to associate sex with feeling unsafe, pain, fear, and disconnection, and this will worsen your relationship cycle. If you're the one who wants to say no to sex with your partner *or* if you're the one who's having trouble hearing no from your partner, refer to the "Talk, Talk, Talk" toolbox section above to work through the encounter together. The best thing you can do for your sex life is have a vulnerable conversation about the emotions around it—not with the goal of changing the outcome, but with the goal of increasing your understanding of your partner and your sense of connection with them.

TOOLS FOR YOUR TOOLBOX:
Change Your Dynamic, Change Your Sex Life!

Okay, back to all the different types of unhealthy sex dynamics! When you notice one of these dynamics kicking into gear, do what *you* can to halt the cycle quickly. You can also use some of the cycle-stopping techniques discussed in chapter 4 about your relationship in general; but here, like there, the first and most important step is recognizing that your negative sex cycle is being set in motion.

Here's a list of all the different sexual dynamics we went over above and quick tips on what you can do to begin to shift your sexual cycle to the secure and connected dynamic we all want.

Unavailable Sex Dynamic:

- Focus on getting emotionally present.

- When you start to notice yourself shutting down emotionally, share with your partner that you are working to get back online.

- Throughout the day, check in with yourself emotionally, working toward learning how to feel your feelings (discussed in chapter 3).

- Gradually attempt to hold on to this awareness and responsiveness when intimately touched by your partner, with a kiss, hug, or snuggle.

- When sex is initiated, try to stay in the sensations of your body, paying attention to your partner's responses and observing how you're interacting.

Makeup Sex Dynamic:

- Diversify the ways in which you and your partner are getting your emotional needs met and having sex. Makeup sex can be part of sexual connection, but you need to have sex without conflict being part of the mix as well.

- Focus on having sex without a fight preceding it.

- When a fight happens, ensure that you both process and emotionally repair the issue first, then have sex.

White-Knuckling It Dynamic:

- Outside the bedroom, share your trauma with your partner when you feel ready. Explain how and why your body reacts the way it does to intimate touch. This will help them realize your reactions are not about them and get you both on the same team.

- Take back your control and remind yourself that you can stop and say no at any time. You don't want to avoid sex, but you also shouldn't white-knuckle through it either—this creates an unsafe sexual dynamic in which you are having sex when you don't want to.

- Understand that your body cannot tell the difference between the past trauma and the safety of the present moment, which is what's causing your resistance.

- When you feel ready, begin with a slow integration of intimacy, like nonsexual touching and then kissing.

- Then proceed slowly through sex, constantly checking in with each other. Remind yourself again that you have the control to stop and say no at any time. The more you experience safe sex, the less reactive your body will be.

- Grant yourself (or your partner) the compassion you deserve for having gone through whatever event generated this type of dynamic in the first place.

- If you've experienced sexual trauma, consider seeking trauma counseling to safely process it.

Freeze Dynamic:

- Outside the bedroom, talk to your partner about how you react when things get physical—it will help them greatly to know it's not rejection or repulsion of them. The more you talk about what causes you to tense up, the more power you take away from it.

- Share the origins of this dynamic with your partner so they can develop empathy and a deeper understanding of it and become more included in the process. You could say, "I care about you, but I need to go slow. In my past, I had to protect myself by eliminating touch. Now my body needs to learn that touch is safe. Can you please help me through this?"

- Tune in to your body to become an expert at noticing your signs before and during freezing moments.

- When you feel triggered, use techniques to regulate your body so you don't fall into this dynamic (see the tools in chapter 3).

- Again, have compassion for yourself for whatever caused you to adopt this dynamic in the first place.

- Get therapy to process past trauma you may have experienced that has contributed to this response.

Anxious/Shame-Based Dynamic:

- Identify your anxious or shame-based negative thought patterns, but remember—your thoughts aren't facts! These are just insecurities.

- Give yourself an affirmation to counter these negative thoughts.

- Seek out a therapist if these negative thoughts feel too daunting to handle on your own. You may have years of insecurities built up that are impairing your sexual arousal.

- To create change, you need to *experience* that you are enough, safe, and lovable. Learn to love yourself and your body.

- Vulnerably share your fears, shame, and anxieties with your partner. They can't understand if you don't explain. Then explicitly ask your partner for reassurance.

"Just Sex" Dynamic:

- Get curious about why you are avoiding deeper intimacy and vulnerable connection. Therapy would be a great place to explore this.

- When you feel ready, practice integrating more intimate actions into sex, such as eye gazing, kissing, and cuddling. Focus on what your partner is experiencing and what you are experiencing in return.

- Tune in to your body to become an expert at noticing signs of shutting out vulnerability and connection. If this becomes triggering, use techniques to regulate your body so you don't fall into this dynamic (see the tools in chapter 3).

Don't Talk About It Dynamic:

- Take the risk of having honest conversations about sex with your partner. Start small—get comfortable with having vulnerable conversations in general first, then build up to being able to talk about sex together. This may take a while and take practice, so just begin by actually naming what you are doing: talking about sex so you can move out of the place where you don't talk about it.

- Consider reading books and watching shows about sex as a launching pad to these conversations.

- Remember that couples who talk about sex have more and better sex—let that be your motivation!

Pursue/Withdraw Dynamic:

- ❂ Each person needs to step outside of their own pattern here in order to stop this dynamic.

- ❂ Those who are withdrawing need to step forward and explain how the pursuing partner's assertive (or aggressive) actions are impacting them, but also acknowledge how their own withdrawal can be negatively impacting the pursuer.

- ❂ Those who are pursuing need to openly share with their partner how the withdrawal makes them feel and also acknowledge how their own pursuit can be negatively impacting their partner.

- ❂ Replace behaviors that are not working (like the not-so-subtle dropped hints and blaming) with vulnerability.

- ❂ Both partners need to show each other that they are loved, desired, valued, and "good enough" in other ways besides sex.

Betrayal Dynamic:

- ❂ If you are the partner who has betrayed in this dynamic, get individual counseling to create healing around the chronic addiction or betrayal you have acted on.

- ❂ If you are the partner having sex in order to save the relationship, recognize this pattern. Acknowledge the unhealthiness of trying to be responsible for your partner's behaviors through having sex. Start therapy to strengthen your self-esteem and honor yourself.

Want more pointers on creating a healthier, more secure sexual dynamic? Visit http://www.newharbinger.com/51932 for our "How to Create Sexual Security" tip sheet.

Be Aware of Your Histories

Throughout this chapter, you've seen some ways in which our personal histories play into our current sexual dynamics, like Miguel's childhood trauma, Julie's molestation, and Peter's religious upbringing. Esther Perel refers to the past emotional histories that impact our adult sexuality now as "erotic blueprints" (2021). These blueprints include our individual understandings and interpretations of concepts like giving, taking, and asking for things from others (Perel 2021; Perel interview 2022). When you're aware of how your past—and your partner's past—influences how you show up in the bedroom now, you can wield this awareness to your advantage.

EXERCISE: What Is Your "Erotic Blueprint"?

Sometimes, our erotic blueprints have conditioned us to be so unaware of our own or others' needs that an important piece of the puzzle in creating a secure sexual dynamic is missing. If we don't know what our needs are, we can't communicate them—so there's no way they're going to get met. The outcome is an unfulfilling sex life with your partner.

In your journal, reflect on the early messages you received about giving, taking, and asking for your needs to be met. How does your history impact your sexuality now? What is your vision of what sex could be like in the future? What do you emotionally and physically need to help you engage sexually?

Next, if you feel emotionally ready, share some of these details of your "erotic blueprint" with your partner. (Refer back to the "How to Share Tender Spots in Three Steps" exercise in chapter 5 for a quick road map on how to do this.) Familiarizing yourself with each other's blueprints is a big step forward in the making of your dream home, founded on a secure attachment, with a secure sexual dynamic.

Tying It All Together

Sex is a sensitive topic—and for good reason. Sexuality is a core aspect of being human, but unfortunately, it is also an aspect that is commonly violated and misunderstood. Our goal in this chapter was to provide you with some concrete information and tools you can use around this vulnerable part of relationships, but we also acknowledge that these tools may not be for everyone at this point in their healing journey.

The most important message is to keep sex emotionally safe for both partners, as feeling secure sexually is critical to a healthy sexual relationship. As you move into your new dream home that you've built together, you'll experience an improved sex life there!

CHAPTER 8

Celebrate, Connect, Advance

Congratulations, you have now reached the last stage of EFT! Whew, you can now take a huge, deep breath. Take a moment to soak in the accomplishment of making it through all the hard work of the previous chapters, in which we have led you through a series of concepts and practices directed at reducing and remedying relationship conflict, integrating all the EFT steps and stages into the daily life of your relationship to make these changes stick. Here, in this final chapter, we will focus on:

- Noticing the new view you have of yourself, your partner, and your relationship

- Further nailing down and integrating the positive moves in your relationship now

- Creating new solutions to old problems that used to trigger the negative cycle

- Establishing rituals and routines with your partner that foster long-term connection

EXERCISE: Temperature Check Revisited

We've come full circle! It's time to do a temperature check again, now that you've proceeded through the EFT process meant to heal your relationship. So, today, right now, in your journal, rate the distress level in your relationship on a scale from 0 to 10 (where 0 = not distressing at all and 10 = very distressing). Now flip to the beginning of your journal to see what number you wrote down when you first started this process in chapter 1. Has your number changed?

Recall that we asked you to give these strategies a good three months before reaching any conclusions, to really see the impact on the volatility in your relationship. If you have engaged in all the content in this book for three months and the volatility has not changed (or even gotten worse), it may be a good time to begin considering whether this relationship is right for you. But we have full confidence in EFT and will proceed on the assumption that things *have* gotten better. If you engaged with the content alone, then allow the celebrations in this chapter to be about your own personal growth, awareness, and determination.

Celebrate the Positives

Let's talk about the power of positive emotion—because who doesn't like to feel good? Therapy and healing must not deal only with the negative emotions. Healing-centered therapy must also deal with the positive things associated with new experiences and growth. Positive expression of emotion has been associated with the following benefits (Lamagna 2022):

- Decreased depression
- Decreased distress
- Increased immune function
- Regulation of negative emotions
- Brain shift out of survival mode
- Increased focus, drive, and reasoning skills

- New perspective on difficult life circumstances

- More flexible thinking and problem solving

- Heightened learning

- Strengthened resilience

- Expanded awareness and growth after experiencing a trauma or a crisis

It's so important to shine a spotlight on what's *going well* in your relationship, not just what's been hampering it. So in this final stage of EFT, we'll be celebrating the changes you have made to stop your negative cycle, create a new positive cycle, take vulnerable risks together, and reach for what you need. This final stage also works to further integrate these changes into your daily life, which is the aim of this chapter's exercises.

EXERCISE: Nailing Down a New Message

In your journal, fill in the blanks of the following sentence—a new positive formula to characterize your side of your positive relationship cycle:

When you _____ [insert positive behavior], it sends me the message _____ [insert positive message], and I feel _____ [insert positive emotion].

Communicate this message to your partner. How did they receive it? If it's an option for you, switch places now and have your partner write out their message to you.

A New, Secure Attachment

One amazing part of reaching this last stage of EFT is that couples begin to see a new story, a new narrative, emerge of each partner and of their

relationship. Here's what it looks like in practice when a couple has graduated through all the stages.

Raquel and Zander's Story

*Raquel and Zander had a typical highly escalated dynamic when they
entered couples therapy. Raquel viewed Zander as not caring about her
at all and being selfish for shutting down and withdrawing from her
during heated moments. Zander viewed Raquel as nagging, critical,
and "crazy" for "freaking out" whenever she was upset. Zander's
shutdown caused Raquel to "up the ante" every time he retreated into
his side of the cycle, becoming even louder and more upset, which
made it harder to be heard and seen by him. Raquel's side of the cycle
caused Zander to retreat farther into his shell under the increased
weight of her criticism. Each of their reactions made the other's stance
more pronounced and worsened their dynamic.*

*After moving through the EFT steps and stages, Raquel and
Zander's story began to change. As they did the work to foster a more
secure attachment, Zander came to see that Raquel wasn't "crazy;" she
was simply hurt and wanted to matter to her husband. Raquel realized
that Zander wasn't selfish and uncaring because he withdrew; he was
just overwhelmed by their escalated interactions and didn't know how
to stop them. Both of them began to change their views of themselves as
hurt individuals who were also capable of cooling off and changing.
Eventually, they began to experience the relationship as a place of
safety and connection, where discussion and resolution were possible.
They learned to take emotional risks with each other.*

*Now, because Raquel's awareness of her internal world is clear,
when she becomes fearful, she talks to Zander in a gentle and
vulnerable way about the emotions she's experiencing and what she
needs from him in that moment. Zander sees her reaching for him and
leans in, knowing he can have a positive impact on the situation. He*

now feels capable of showing up for her. And when Zander becomes fearful that conflict is brewing between them, he reaches for Raquel and lets her know what's going on for him in a way that lets her see how important she is to him. He is able to ask her for what he needs emotionally in those moments.

Raquel and Zander now both *experience* the relationship as characterized by A.R.E.—encompassing accessibility, responsiveness, and engagement—so there's no more need to shift into fight-or-flight mode to protect themselves from danger. You may notice here how this couple's story, their view of the other person, themselves, and the relationship, changed as their attachment became more secure. You can do the same thing. As you move away from an old narrative and write a new positive story, you will continue to notice, highlight, integrate, and celebrate the changes in your cycle.

EXERCISE: Writing a New Story

In your journal, complete the following prompts with responses that have occurred since you started this book. What changes have you noticed? They can be big or small.

- ⮞ List three things that you've seen as positive strengths in yourself as you have navigated the contents of this book. Now list three of your partner's strengths that you've witnessed.

- ⮞ List three times you and your partner have had success in stopping your negative cycle and talked in a more vulnerable way that kept you both close.

- ⮞ List three examples of when you and your partner have been A.R.E. for each other.

- ⮞ List three things you now have hope for in your relationship for the future.

This is proof that you can do it, proof that positive change is happening! Share this proof with your partner and see what they have to add. Then keep this journal entry close whenever you are feeling overwhelmed, frustrated, or triggered by hard emotions. Use these observations as an anchor to remind yourself of the growth in your relationship. Refer back to these lists again and again as you continue to work on your relationship. You've got this!

Taking Risks and Creating New Cycles

In this final stage, we begin noticing couples taking new emotional risks with each other that they wouldn't have before. This is a beautiful thing because it invites more vulnerability into the relationship, and it also invites each partner to have a different reaction to new behaviors. It births a new, positive cycle in the relationship that begins to blossom with the effects of positivity: as one partner interacts with the other in a new, positive way, this elicits a more positive response from the partner, which in turn creates a more positive response from the other ... and on and on it goes. The creation of a new cycle!

EXERCISE: Taking Risks

In your journal, write down three to five instances in your relationship since starting this book when you took a risk with your partner *that you normally wouldn't have before.* Did you share a primary emotion with them? Maybe you called out your cycle at the beginning of an argument last month? Or maybe you invited them on a date last weekend? Both big and small risks can have a significant impact on the relationship, so nothing is too minor to consider. Remember, taking risks with your partner is so important because that's what leads to the new positive cycle you're creating.

Now explore how your partner reacted in these three to five examples. Were they A.R.E. with you? How do these reactions influence the likelihood of you continuing to take risks like this with them in the future?

EXERCISE: Establishing Your New Positive Cycle

Remember when you identified the elements of your negative cycle in chapter 4? We're going to do the same thing here, but this time, with a positive twist! Get out your trusty journal and fill in the blanks!

The more I _____ [insert positive behavior], the more my partner feels _____ [insert emotion] and responds by _____ [insert positive behavior].

In response, the more I _____ [insert behavior].

Underneath, this makes me feel _____ [insert emotion].

And my partner feels _____ [insert emotion].

Here's an example of what this can look like in the newly constructed positive cycle of a couple that has graduated from EFT:

The more I turn toward my partner with vulnerability and share my emotions and my fears, the more my partner feels safe with me and responds by opening up more themselves.

In response, the more I come closer to them.

Underneath, this makes me feel loved and safe.

And my partner feels good enough and happy.

Out with the Old and in with the New

Another great benefit of reaching this stage of EFT: new solutions to old problems begin to emerge for a couple. Let's revisit Zander and Raquel to illustrate what we mean.

One of the issues that Zander and Raquel brought into couples therapy was Zander's relationship with his mother, whom Raquel doesn't get along with. Zander and his mom have always been close, and she is someone he will turn to during difficult moments in his life—including fights with

Raquel. This would infuriate Raquel, and she'd rage at him for his insensitivity, which ironically only drew Zander closer to his mother for her sympathy and support.

Underneath Raquel's anger, the soft, vulnerable primary emotions she was feeling were tremendous sadness, loneliness, and painful rejection from the person she wanted connection with the most. But Zander couldn't see that through all Raquel's taunts and accusations; all he could see was her disappointment in him. This made him cherish having his mother as his confidante even more—not only was she a safe place to turn to when things were tough at home, but also her advice actually gave him hope that he could figure out a way to "fix things" with his wife or make the fighting stop.

Through EFT, Zander became aware of Raquel's longing to be close to him, for *her* to be the safe place he turned to in times of need. And Raquel became aware of Zander's longing for a peaceful connection with her and his need to have some control over making things better in their relationship.

Now they don't fight about his mom anymore. When they do disagree and the triggers do come up (trust us, they still will, for any couple), it's no longer a fight. Instead, it's a conversation focused, not on Zander's mother, but on the underlying emotional process and the couple's attachment needs. They turn toward each other and show up for each other now.

Raquel will say to Zander, "Hey, babe, I'm feeling really disconnected and scared you're going to turn away from me. Can we take a moment to reconnect here? I just need to feel close to you right now and get some reassurance that you know you can confide in me."

And Zander will say to Raquel, "Hey, babe, I'm feeling really nervous about this turning into a conflict. I don't want to fall into our old pattern of disconnecting. Can we cool things down together? I want to stay close to you in this moment and get this right with you."

EXERCISE: Devising New Solutions

In your journal, explore the following questions, then consider sharing with your partner. If they're up for it, invite them to answer the questions from their perspective too.

- What new solutions to your "old problems" in the relationship are you now emerging with?

- What has helped you get to these new solutions?

- If new solutions don't quite exist yet, what do you think you need in order to create new solutions to these old problems?

Relationship Rituals

World-famous relationship researchers John and Julie Gottman coined the term "rituals of connection." In their work, the Gottmans discuss the importance of couples creating meaningful, informal (how you greet each other, for example), and formal (holidays, for example) rituals as a way of building a strong, successful, and lasting relationship (Gottman and Gottman 2000–2012). Rituals are a way for a couple to create a deep sense of shared meaning in their life together.

From an EFT perspective, they continue to foster and strengthen the secure bond you've been working so hard on. Creating these formal and informal rituals, though, can be tough and time-consuming to set in place, and they can be easy to forget to maintain amid the chaos of everyday life. So here's the trick to establishing a successful, intentional ritual of connection: it has to be reliable, consistent, realistic, and sustainable in your current context. For example, if you have a new baby, setting up a ritual of connection that pledges you will have a one-on-one date night every week is not a realistic expectation, so it can easily lead to disappointment.

So when looking for consistent and manageable rituals, think about something you can do every morning (like make sure to kiss each other goodbye), every night before bed (share something you're grateful for from your day), or on Sunday evenings (have a movie night with cuddling and popcorn). As you begin to trust the safety of this predictable and dependable addition to your daily life, your secure attachment will become further cemented into the foundation of your new dream home.

We (Jennine and Jacqueline) both have intentional rituals of connection with our partners that we have integrated into our lives. One of them is what the Gottmans call a "state of the union meeting." During these regular check-ins, we discuss with our partners how things have been going in the relationship, how we are each feeling individually, any emotional needs we are having, any ruptures in the relationship that need repair, and, of course, what's going well (never forget to focus on the positives!). Because we both have children, we have to schedule these check-ins when time allows us to have them, like over coffee in the morning or before we get out of bed on slower weekend mornings.

Creating shared rituals requires planning and intentionality—and it's totally worth it. It creates a time and a place where you can connect and interact meaningfully. It keeps the conversations about vulnerability and attachment needs flowing. It keeps the *two of you* flowing, surrounded by the three components of A.R.E. and consistently adding new materials to your healthy, lasting relationship.

EXERCISE: Picking a Ritual

What can you and your partner regularly do to create intentional connection time? Jot down a handful of ideas in your journal and then share them with your partner. Work together to pick just one ritual to start with—something you can realistically do on a consistent basis—and have fun with it! We recommend blocking this same time off on your calendar to make sure you fulfill the commitment and not making the ritual too complicated—if it's too hard to maintain, it will fall away.

Tying It All Together

This is what psychologist Diana Fosha has to say about the paramount importance of our relationship to a significant other: "The roots of resilience...are to be found in the sense of being understood by and existing in the mind and heart of a loving, attuned, and self-possessed other" (quoted in Van der Kolk 2015, 107). We can't think of a better way to summarize the essence of our work together throughout this book. It takes great resilience to stay in it with someone you love when things are very difficult, to hold on to hope, to fight for things to get better.

But now look at you! You are working on your new relationship as trapeze artists side by side together: communicating clearly where you are, breathing through your fear, jumping with vulnerability, sharing genuine emotions, reaching for what you need, and catching each other. You will both take turns as flyer and catcher in the act, because that's what it means to reciprocate, love, understand, and show up.

We are so proud of you for getting to this stage of the EFT process, where you fully and authentically exist in the mind and heart of your partner and where they exist in yours. We want you to know that you exist in our minds and hearts as well, and we thank you for your trust. We have dedicated our lives to understanding the nuances, complexities, and beauty that all form the messiness of the human relational experience, and it is from this experience that resilience grows.

We know the hard work you put into getting to this point and we applaud you for it, but the work isn't over. Even if you've fully moved into your new home and it's decorated to your liking, you now have to maintain it, to dedicate continual upkeep. As you do so, you should come back to this book—any part of this book—anytime you need to. Going through the stages we just traversed isn't meant to be a one-time trip. It's an approach and a lifestyle, a relationship lifestyle, that should be revisited over and over, keeping your sights on the "emotionally focused" part of EFT.

We hope this book has served and will continue to serve as a conduit toward a deeper, more connected relationship for the two of you and that you are now beginning to truly feel the joy of healing that comes from being understood by and existing in the mind and heart of a loving, attuned, and self-possessed partner.

Afterword

Practical and intensely engaging, *Help for High-Conflict Couples* is a gold mine for any couple struggling in their relationship. Not only does this book detail the most vital aspects of attachment theory and integration of emotionally focused therapy, but it also outlines the journey each couple takes as they enter into the fight for their lives.

Jennine Estes and Jacqueline Wielick are powerfully compassionate and insightful authors who reach to the heart of the matter for each partner who is painfully stuck in a high-conflict dynamic. Each chapter provides exercises for the couple to explore their contribution to the conflicts and then very clear next steps if they are both committed to restoring a secure relationship. The biggest impact this book will have on all couples around the globe is the intimacy it provides for readers—in these pages, they can find themselves, they can access a place where they feel seen and understood, where they are not alone.

If you were thinking about taking your partner to therapy, reading this book will give you more hope for your future and predictability around the emotionally focused therapy treatment process.

This book is not just for couples; it should be read by all couples therapists who strive to be excellent clinicians. The story lines tied in with what is, in my opinion, the premier marital therapy model available today bring depth and understanding to working with high-conflict relationships in a way that no other book has done before.

I know this contribution to the field of couples therapy will be referenced for years to come.

—Lisa J. Palmer-Olsen, PsyD, LMFT,
EFT TrainerCodirector and Founder
of Renova San Diego

References

Abramson, A. 2020. "If There Was Ever a Time to Activate Your Vagus Nerve, It Is Now." *Elemental*, April 10. https://elemental.medium.com/if-there-was-ever-a-time-to-activate-your-vagus-nerve-it-is-now-2227e8c6885b.

Barhash, E. 2017. "Different Types of Trauma: Small 't' versus Large 'T.'" *Psychology Today*, March 13. https://www.psychologytoday.com/us/blog/trauma-and-hope/201703/different-types-trauma-small-t-versus-large-t.

Bowlby, J. 1982. *Attachment and Loss. Volume 1: Attachment.* 2nd ed. New York: Basic Books. https://mindsplain.com/wp-content/uploads/2020/08/ATTACHMENT_AND_LOSS_VOLUME_I_ATTACHMENT.pdf.

Bretherton, I. 1992. "The Origins of Attachment Theory: John Bowlby and Mary Ainsworth." *Developmental Psychology* 28(5): 759–775.

Cannon, W. B. 1932. *The Wisdom of the Body.* New York: W. W. Norton, 177–201. Referenced in Wikipedia, n.d. "Walter Bradford Cannon." Accessed July 8, 2022. https://en.wikipedia.org/w/index.php?title=Walter_Bradford_Cannon&oldid=1145150197.

Cassidy, J., J. D. Jones, and P. R. Shaver. 2013. "Contributions of Attachment Theory and Research: A Framework for Future Research, Translation, and Policy." *Development and Psychopathology* 25(4 pt. 2): 1415–1434.

Chapman, G. D. 1995. *The Five Love Languages: How to Express Heartfelt Commitment to Your Mate*. Chicago: Northfield Publishing.

Gehart, D. 2014. *Theory and Treatment Planning in Family Therapy: A Competency-Based Approach*. Boston: Cengage Learning.

Goldman, J. 2010. "Ed Tronick and the 'Still Face Experiment.'" *Scientific American*, October 18. https://blogs.scientificamerican .com/thoughtful-animal/ed-tronick-and-the-8220-still-face -experiment-8221.

Gottman, J. M. 2011. *The Science of Trust: Emotional Attunement for Couples*. New York: W. W. Norton.

Gottman, J., and J. S. Gottman. 2000–2012. *Level 1 Clinical Training: Gottman Method Couples Therapy. Bridging the Couple Chasm, Home Study Training Manual*. The Gottman Institute. https://www .gottman.com/product/gottman-method-couples-therapy-level-1.

Johnson, S. 2008. *Hold Me Tight: Seven Conversations for a Lifetime of Love*. New York: Little, Brown.

Johnson, S. 2013. *Externships in Emotionally Focused Couples Therapy: Participants Manual*. San Diego: International Center for Excellence in Emotionally Focused Therapy.

Johnson, S., and P. Greenman. 2013. "Commentary: Of Course It Is All About Attachment!" *Journal of Marital and Family Therapy* 39(4): 421–423.

Johnson, S. M., and J. A. Makinen. 2006. "Resolving Attachment Injuries in Couples Using Emotionally Focused Therapy: Steps Towards Forgiveness and Reconciliation." *Journal of Consulting and Clinical Psychology* 74(6): 1055–1064.

Johnson, S. M., J. A. Makinen, and J. W. Millikin. 2001. "Attachment Injuries in Couple Relationships: A New Perspective on Impasses in Couples Therapy." *Journal of Marital and Family Therapy* 27(2): 145–155.

Johnson, S. M., Z. Simakhodskaya, and M. Moran. 2018. "Addressing Issues of Sexuality in Couples Therapy: Emotionally Focused Therapy Meets Sex Therapy." *Current Sexual Health Reports* 10: 65–71.

Kallos-Lilly, V., and J. Fitzgerald. 2015. *An Emotionally Focused Workbook for Couples.* New York: Routledge.

Lamagna, J. 2022. "AEDP Immersion" (live online course). AEDP Institute. https://aedpinstitute.org/aedp-training/immersion-course.

Obegi, J. H., and E. Berant, eds. 2009. *Attachment Theory and Research in Clinical Work with Adults.* New York: Guilford Press.

Palmer-Olsen, L. 2022. Personal interview with authors.

Perel, E. 2021. "Bringing Home the Erotic: 5 Ways to Create Meaningful Connections with Your Partner." EsterPerel.com. https://www.estherperel.com/blog/5-ways-to-create-meaningful -connections.

PsychAlive. 2018. "Dr. Stephen Porges: What Is the Polyvagal Theory." https://www.youtube.com/watch?v=ec3AUMDjtKQ.

Raghunathan, R. 2014. "The Need to Love." *Psychology Today,* January 8. https://www.psychologytoday.com/us/blog/sapient-nature /201401/the-need-love.

Raypole, C. 2021. "The Beginner's Guide to Trauma Responses." *Healthline,* August 26. https://www.healthline.com/health/mental -health/fight-flight-freeze-fawn#the-basics.

Recovery Direct. n.d. "To Treat Trauma, Tone the Vagus Nerve." Accessed October 13, 2022. https://www.recoverydirect.co.za /to-treat-trauma-tone-the-vagus-nerve.

Rees, C. 2007. "Childhood Attachment." *British Journal of General Practice* 57(544): 920–922.

Roe, T. n.d. "Nervous System Regulation Tools." https://drive.google .com/file/d/1drLehMmbo5lkTFNiTxnGj_99NhD4CVmr/view.

Slootmaeckers, J., and L. Migerode. 2019. "EFT and Intimate Partner Violence: A Roadmap to De-escalating Violent Patterns." *Family Process*. Wiley Online Library. https://onlinelibrary.wiley.com/doi/abs/10.1111/famp.12468.

van der Kolk, Bessel. 2015. *The Body Keeps the Score: Brain, Mind, and Body in the Healing of Trauma.* New York: Penguin.

Weizmann, F. 2001. "Edward John Mostyn Bowlby (1907–1990)." *Psychologist* 14(9): 465. https://www.proquest.com/docview/211829376/939964273FE749E4PQ/1.

"What Your Upbringing Says About Who You Are in Bed." 2002. Interview with Esther Perel on Goop.com. https://goop.com/wellness/sexual-health/upbringing-says-bed.

Wiebe, S. A., and S. M. Johnson. 2016. "A Review of the Research in Emotionally Focused Therapy for Couples." *Family Process* 55(3): 390–407.

Witter, I. 2017. "Emotionally Focused Therapy for Emotionally Escalated Couples." *San Diego Psychologist*, June 30. https://thesandiegopsychologist.com/2017/06/30/emotionally-focused-therapy-for-emotionally-escalated-couples.

Woolley, S. 2022. Personal interview with authors.

Jennine Estes Powell, LMFT, is founder of Estes Therapy, a group practice in San Diego, CA, that concentrates on relationship counseling. As a licensed marriage and family therapist who is certified in emotionally focused therapy (EFT), she has been helping countless couples repair their rifts and reinvigorate their connection for more than twenty years. She also trains other therapists and serves as a mentor for colleagues. Her aim is to strategically apply empirically based techniques to create positive, long-term change. Learn more at www.estestherapy.com.

Jacqueline Wielick, LMFT, is a licensed marriage and family therapist and owner of her own private practice, Therapy by Jackie. She has a master of science in marriage and family therapy, and degrees in both psychology and sociology. With a focus on couples, relationships, attachment, trauma, and emotions, Jackie's passion is helping people find deep joy in themselves and in their relationships using her advanced training in research-based theories such as EFT and Gottman Method Couples Therapy. Jackie previously worked at The Gottman Institute for five years, one of the world's leading research institutes for couples and relationships, where she was exposed to their revolutionary research on love and relationships. Learn more at www.jackiewielick.com.

Real change *is* possible

For more than forty-five years, New Harbinger has published proven-effective self-help books and pioneering workbooks to help readers of all ages and backgrounds improve mental health and well-being, and achieve lasting personal growth. In addition, our spirituality books offer profound guidance for deepening awareness and cultivating healing, self-discovery, and fulfillment.

Founded by psychologist Matthew McKay and Patrick Fanning, New Harbinger is proud to be an independent, employee-owned company. Our books reflect our core values of integrity, innovation, commitment, sustainability, compassion, and trust. Written by leaders in the field and recommended by therapists worldwide, New Harbinger books are practical, accessible, and provide real tools for real change.

 newharbingerpublications

MORE BOOKS from
NEW HARBINGER PUBLICATIONS

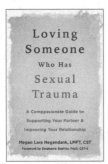

Did you know there are **free tools** you can download for this book?

Free tools are things like **worksheets, guided meditation exercises**, and **more** that will help you get the most out of your book.

You can download free tools for this book— whether you bought or borrowed it, in any format, from any source—from the New Harbinger website. All you need is a NewHarbinger.com account. Just use the URL provided in this book to view the free tools that are available for it. Then, click on the "download" button for the free tool you want, and follow the prompts that appear to log in to your NewHarbinger.com account and download the material.

You can also save the free tools for this book to your **Free Tools Library** so you can access them again anytime, just by logging in to your account! Just look for this button on the book's free tools page. ➤ **+ Save this to my free tools library**

If you need help accessing or downloading free tools, visit **newharbinger.com/faq** or contact us at **customerservice@newharbinger.com.**